THE RED BOOK
OF
HERGEST WARD

RHYS TRIMBLE

NEWTON-LE-WILLOWS

Published in the United Kingdom in 2018
by The Knives Forks And Spoons Press,
51 Pipit Avenue,
Newton-le-Willows,
Merseyside,
WA12 9RG.

ISBN 978-1-912211-17-3

Acknowledgments:

Some of these poems have appeared in *Zarf* and *Datableed.*

Table of Contents / Cynnwys

Introduction to *The Red Book of Hergest Ward*

This is a sequence of what I retrospectively regard as 'countersonnets', and they are composed from overheard and gathered material. They derive their shape from the floorplan of the Hergest Unit in Bangor, Gwynedd. The Hergest Unit consists of 3 octagonal buildings that are named after the poets Taliesin, Cynan and Aneurin. A number of my friends have been temporarily housed at this department of Ysbyty Gwynedd Hospital over the years.

The Red Book of Hergest, which provides much of the material for this book, is a Middle Welsh text scribed by Hywel Fychan and others in the fourteenth century. It contains seminal Welsh works of literature, including 'The Mabinogion' and the poetry of 'Y Cynfeirdd' and 'Y Gogynferidd'.

Cych

Cwm Cych in South Wales is the supposed location for the gateway to Annwn (the otherworld), and it is the setting for the *Mabinogi* story 'Pwyll Pendefig Dyfed'. This sequence is a psychomythogeographical attempt to find the entrance to Annwn using only a map of the Kiev Metro for reference. Texts from numerous visits to Cwm Cych were collaged and edited using a Markov Chain Genorator. A Markov chain generator selects combinations of letters or words based on the original state of the text. Setting a Markov Chain Generator at a low order will allow the fusion of fragments of words, based on their order or state, in the original text input. This leaves a trace of the source text used, however minimal or mathematically conceptual in the output text. The resultant neologisms were then augmented by a purposeful 'neologism generator', created by Tom Jenks, which has been modified to create combinations of Welsh and English suffixes and prefixes to create Welsh-English hybrid words or 'colliderings'.

Branwen 18 Ways

18 constraints, both newly devised and Oulipian, were employed to treat the text from the *Mabinogi* story 'Branwen Ferch Llyr' to create the 18 cantos. Edwards John Morgan's *Mabinogion: O Lyfr Coch Hergest* (1921) was used as a starting point here, and then the text

from one section is passed onto the next, or sometimes passed back to earlier versions in the chain of 18. This process is similar to that employed by Raymond Queneau in *Exercices de Style* (1947), which also echoes the scribal methodology for creating a compendium of works such as the *Red Book of Hergest*.

IV Membranaceous in Folio

For this section I used the Universal Transverse Mercator Coordinate System to gather the Geodetic Datum (longitude / latitude coordinates) for the following locations: the Hergest Unit in Bangor; Hergest Court in Hereford, where the book was kept in a private library for many years; and the Bodleian Library in Oxford, where the book currently resides. This produced the coordinates 52°11'30.57"N -33°12'18"W, 53°12'25.4412"N -49°39'08"W, and 51°45' 15.5226"N -11°51'51.41"W. These number sequences were used to select passages from the original manuscript for *The Red Book of Hergest*. These passages were then translated from Middle Welsh using various methods: a homophonic translation, which preserved some of the phonological sounds of the original; a semantic translation, where I felt confident in my understanding of the text and where I was able to preserve the syntax of the original; and by using Google Translate in conjunction with spell check in Word to suggest amusing alternatives. Line breaks have been altered somewhat to create a more readable poetry. Some sections appear to have been selected twice – by accident. Much of the text appears to be from the Trojan Wars written by Dares Phrygius found in Welsh in the Original MS. Some general vocabulary is repeated sufficiently to provoke me to provide a small glossary. The resultant is Wealish, a 'spectrum language' varying syntactically between English and Welsh. This is meant to be read aloud as sound poetry.

THE RED BOOK
OF
HERGEST WARD

sonnets / rooms

compounded {adj} {past-p} hergestellt
manufactured {adj} {past-p}hergestellt
made {adj} {past-p}hergestellt
fashioned {adj} {past-p}hergestellt
produced {adj} {past-p}hergestellt
constructed {adj} {past-p}hergestellt

for Nancy

a

grandfathers' mumble became whitenoise
hum & violet, plutonian but place
direct told right thru childish
this is an experiment
of site "and foretime
gibberish & wreck bar beats echochamber
prehistoricity & what is exertine
"the adaptations, the fusions
the transmogrifications-but always
inward continuities?
is is
of this site
of place
"leidr gogledd heddiw"
&
hywel ab owain
Gwynedd reborn though a line slipped
on her pregancy test i
was least & paramount of
all techniques older; things
portmanteau words palimpsestical
i was right that day, correct
universal is english – that i
wanted to say things (history
that that that that that that had had
may god repay the adjutants of my
spent years pretending invalidity, valid decreasing disparity crushed parts
only to find yourself vital on work
& high on aggregate & shovelling
modern simile a flavour of icecream
rum & raisin, pink gin, pink skin gin ju-ju
arch & the man from saturn
saturnalia & saturnine, sun-ra
fuck-me on kindle &

fathers doing
orderly things

pruritic concup
iscence luck & inter
necine, a good honey
moon apart from the per
sonel

2

bedlam & tom o'bedlam
crie wise loki'ed because
insane & dunsinane on their heads
"put them away"

THE RED BOOK

IS

BEDLAM

metromania

&

the hour of

masturbation

THE

BLACK

MONTH

Kandinsky's triangle   apollo
Wasily—"it came to me in an
erection, dog dreams & brevity-cut
all up & synaptic cut syntactic
is chunks of pedagogy listen to
what is said; bicycle-up hardness &
o-ring was gasket—we know these
techniques; we know these techniques
we know these techniques; nothing wrong
with direction—in each thing it's opposite
think fewer & i love you I SAY I SAY

iii

radicalization punters on pdf
wait, smash-up bus-stops & freer
tubed & mapped & knowledge is
unused but forced golden showers &
golden veins is lay is VANILLA fu
ck the masons fugu Allah akbar not know
Al-Aqsa "render the middle classes
torpid with ennui through selective
radio 4 scheduling" high sideral strung
transport vee hickle: a broken bulldog clip rumble, halftimbered town fivish
i drove out here, but have nothing to do
probably i will find a thousand classes of
which when they sit down to, will not do
anything, myddfai meddyg too much
longevity ri-anladh-glossography,
rhizophora topological is symbol, big &
theoretical needs higgs' boson bison by
mindmap of histomystical spacetime hope yellow dogparticle capstone &
& how were they superiour godspeck particular, anterior, flawed? dragnet UBIQ
attenuated duty ich dien pattern
recog. a surl development pun
punk – diy hole kiss the same old
faces, good guestimator, will back
seat aesthetic slide, sexual timidity
figura etymologica LLOERDORRI moonstroke
on corrugated plastic a quantized poem

d

& how do you know if it's
knowingly done—faith, god, GOBAITH
& to misunderstand is to know, meinhir
altitudinal while stripe blaen-ffrancon
dis-chime more cross out syntagm, hail
descendants of the vanguard— HENFFYCH!
ac felly but when i was young I tried to comprehend
the view; "you gotta see the car to call
shotgun—that's the rules of shotgun"

Kanys hynny a uydei glotuaɞr y uilɞryaeth ef.
A gɞedy clybot o Jason ymadraɞd y brenhin
megys ydoed deɞr ef ac ymynnei ef gɞybot
deuodeu pob lle kanys ef adebygei yuot
ynglotuorussach rac llaɞ beidyckei efy dreis
yr hɞrd ar croen eureit o ynys colcos. Ac yna

fe'i redefines good::good & excoriate
is a word i learnt *   [grey areas]
a series of thefts— ad asterisk ad silvam
trapped words from   science come &
considered & in parts ∞, 0 algebra
e=natural number=filtration through
a zillion arseholes & distended conc
iousness, small cogs—chose to live
by pop-ballads system exceeds
poetry & shame & poetry & shame
circling, extirpate lux, gole tywyll / dark
romance of the jobcenre—bedlam universalé

V

tyranny of the moral – wish you were yur
but you're not – "pela cascara"
"i bought
it from an asian wideboy in Bury" people
are annhiliators, ca-catylysts & sounders
english is postkepi & late, tongue of t/win
ning - a double rotary helicopter flies
overhead—plastic with hallucinations
we are free to walk on the A55
(playing marbles) yayarbles korybski
real skiing is slippery"[the] few & less of poetry—
rhwng haln, padded or unpadded?— between events i was
illegitimate [ABUSIVE] unsanctioned DEAD GULL
DEAD GULL; DEAD GULL; sweatedge
Fish fin slippered love all meat
& onions white horse of hope Pen-y-pas
well ghent! peripotent my pellucid queen
a belt for Barry (48") conservativerefers
to jam? portents for Nancy—my latent
orderedness—"little practical
chap" one letter, number in postcode, map terri
tory relation o topo, el, ek-ology of mind
& theology of alcoholics anonymous supertasks
jermyn st, maid to measure papa wemba,
pink corduroy – the word is place &
territorial jingo, l ogue explicate in unuus, inte
grate; @ the burger van (guard) that has had
some of the journeyman's art (izzen) turf &
serf. self-igniting pistol, her-guestellt pun-sex
pak-minster-by-right no rite, confiscation
of tendencies, Bethan cuts herself

vi

& thank you for teaching me inviolate
or inerotic passing notes on my behalf & i was sad
for her, conceit & trick vagina, christfox
delete my dick-picture bulwark hwch & faith
elf botherer, marshall-plur-valve-amp rinky
dink imaginary lenses – a chargeless mote
red is the colour of warning unless you're
colourblind like a dog." coch, cochyn corach
this place with its mundane lacerations, this
location ll a name which cannot be pronounced
by telephone, calendrical impositions, lives

part of the morning's duties was separating cop
ulating men." opportunely romances as exp
eriment, o nadja! one syllable & punnet
punitive - one does what one does- [the] soft
rubric of a vee dub engine as a young wo
man [i don't say girl] walks by with a scarlet
violin on her back - we all know thought as
messy - archipel fractal zonzo, sgidie chwarel
out buildings resemble exonyms – the first stone
that emerged from the chaos & well hench
we rip open pillows & scaphoid, scapulae
& sick doctors & tripleancies – scrofulous

7

transhumance & transurance playing ludo with
ludites, homo ludus divulge kamen
vortex street walker is putting one foot in front
of another [not ritual] [not symbol] AUDIENCE
PROVOCATEUR   BOOM BOOM BOOM!
cherry picker tall & immerse sept into the fuck
ing vulgar – presentation & within brack
ets ish & isms "ow we speak; red fingers
are genetic – COIN vestigial RECULVER
EXIT INTERVIEW cacography DEFOD
                                        specie, running fight, linoleum palace &
                                        always circular within circe, vicarious
                                        vicious vicar's daughter – you inherit   what you
                                        built a bag of monies, a purse's pwrs moment thread
                                        ing one vector vek & flyaway spheric nomad
                                        beat short circuit endocrine poetry spurt &
                                        & gleaming spires hindbrain & chris pineal
                                        [bushell] of winter blanks, black &
                                        tralalalatitious quidnunc & free veins fetish
                                        misdemeanours vivre exchange genitalia on
ogham phones qua qua a series of nearly unnoticeable
people with sufficient energy – le jetty
promontary haversack motorcycle courier & jade xmas
love & burgeon bedlam site become mind
rows of "uprights" – you feel like taking risks
on risky days: like-on-like & likeminded just
ice becomes a hangover is a disease of the
eyes like a wine taster's pallette i am xmas
not one for writing things down right by
rational & offset a little "sitting down by
a fire, a wanking dog, a dancing bear

h

onanorous night hunting text as i become poli
tical becoming right mistakes & ogive
who knows but to drift misuse fertility by
& knows who palpates – fleisch water disturb
or mould but this is my face

to
who

drifts

lizardess (Gaz)

one thing stands for another thing, gains
meat becomes another whispering
sidgilus "y gair" nid lor nac olrhain
Iesu and (oblegid Duw) hanes cerdd
neu sain – llythren bu farw ∂ er eng
raifft nid sarff yn cnoi' cynffon efallai dda
w eraill ar f'ôl—gen i ffydd yn ffff ac ssss
irresolute tiger membrane between
languages between meyou cockcunt &&
now the burning cigar end viewed thru
a telescope burn through this page on to
time—the right person YOU YOU YOU

adult attenuated, adult attenuated, hoodied
& holt, everything neatly separated by greaseproof
paper hoying down dialect bisgedyn penwan [wyllt] hwch
freda erzuli en tapis noir carded danger
eux by maesonic 4 mesostic confluence elder
& eldritch by fakelips i pervade duwch
bol buwch, tywallt eurlaw nadoligaidd [the]
strength of the insane uh uh institution

alized, cynan gwalchmai hergest talwrn
wallgof oi coia beirdd na ddefnyddir eiriau
sgwenna i calon i"r sawdl: saith camau
lle ordovici neu tanteingl, yma::bolahaul

9

strawberry thief, you imagined purple space
suit – experiment with christ, elvis &&&
supspecies yourself selfsame familiar
repaired my create   with a rash, deny your
fire & fake lusts – i wouldn't be move
d by my fire"– micro, picoscopic atoms or
cell-slide rough event horizon, british
blondes, lizardess, lisabet prophylactic
supple health & abakwa LLYFR GWYN
verité-llwy llefain neu agribuzz, fferm a thyddyn
[the] most numerous of farms [magazine] y tocyn cochyn/ ginger rover it, will
get thirsty at times" [the living card]
arts & crafts, kilowatt hours – all wyse-
neuron drone cities straight eight path &
lighthouse "a shadow i mistook for a path
space between beats & whitenoise seastriated
ritual a dogwalking circuit" female sanity
"star this significance, stellated – give the gift
you'll be dead before you know it [...] "some
thing grows to replace the hole, hergest is
liked, a spiked wheel down this spoke, corridor
scrimmages of mysogyno-creeps-down-this
thunner pash & explain regret to mercury I
write out what is hidden – those buried concrete
steps"– lighthouse keepers are automatons now
o robotinik, spiderman vs jesus coming ireation
"those cultural signs of intelligence" radiospeaking
i like the way other people do things ... journeys ...
planning infidelities ... difficult pleasantries ... un
reliable recorder-bethan hurts herself but hits
body made blush & it's one of the skills you
gave me – working out whether you're drunk
or not – llyma diwedd y trydet geinc

X

6 sodium moons=paracystosis, welsh aedeology erebus
erebus overdressed for bethesda, an abortive
notation denoting time - difficult as a micmick
to see WHAT I AM admiration – cyn diwedd
y noson cyscwyt gen hi"
illiterate nanation, hand
@hannah sin water hase
excrescence, ac fellu bu
seeming right, silver
& galvanized in zinc to read
sometimes heavy, sometimes light, venting waste
emotions – fe cyrchant hyd Dyfet deny your heritage – get status dog, twelve
gulleys man, cyrchasant hyd lloegr – my
great-grandfather was a taylor – konnecting disp
arate patches – scandal! plenary plenum the
cap'd year – all is inviolate, up for grabs
crecy in blut, moreso & y mae gwithien aur –
sef y llwybr, jones & peglar its all up 4 grabs
each orange light a territory (allfather) lite cart
ography [the] biblical has wept into your he
art & tip edge-murder metaphor choc
–olate indulgence like how you excuse male
foundering in snow, raveline aleatory fuck ups
sparx, zoo time its me & youtime diplotemyga
[expletives not deleted] CUNT love strut & small
marks have big trails big 'distal clouds' id &
visual jokes make bitterns laugh, sad
junkie scum [poetry] [...] an elegant charlatry
come see me dance between sideral morae
lity, chancery or sideways & corsetry
human interest is inserted here. point
A/B & UNIT philosophy intrigues

k

off-licence poetry—fascinated by the
oretical workings of her own body – sic Nancy is
a little god today : – forcing the world
morning is full of largess, the shame assoc
iated with my dog shitting i record what i
remember to pull down & what i don't , series
copyists, cabla of sheep – llechu dan goed
handless manufacture – lock paws! its raining
[the] slates are clean, llanlleifiad o ent
omancey VERITAS TEMPORIS FILIA forgive
& forget " that's quit the world you live in

pulled apart my heartset, sett glitchy, punkchild
wayne county & the electric chairs ... rats & delicious
palatate! supersymmetry vocoder neck
tube CLR james connexions [sp!] [sp!] [sp!] a
woman walking a long a track, the
"Hergest Unit promises to treat all their
clients as individuals and to give credence
to their individuality, creed, race or religion"
live evil. portraiture   in smoke – Kigua
& Rhiannon // promote the social aspects of
dining. spent force. borealopithicine dancers

xii

balletic or recitative – & what called you
to me & shaped your absence ... think rar
e&my teeth against yours & fingers tight on
[a] grip—missing my boy/girl, can you feel the
dew on your forearms, hunker down in
the went woods ... when you're backs to
the wall resort to bromance – pistal drawn band
olier & gauze; o moment is my omitance
multiplication; a year turns astophysical
draumaturgy rupture rates, arableague &
armed insurgency-bat for lashes

the lord of the underworld is concerning him
self with tearing up cheeswrappers" yan tan
tethera methera—left lyricism reclaim
fingertips—bent them to your torque; torc, trust
my veins & explicate insanity, inside myself
all this is a lie & survey of use
lessness – the red eye month, not demons
but crying; you'd really be beautiful if
you were white" so in blood – smash [the]
sea with my body, baroreceptors, Llŷr Beli

13

i stood in for someone with black hair, new
year, coal & her dynasty of chickpeas, too muc
h control done it; wrench-red slate, red anthracite
mutton & places always on my fingernails, Uncle
Hergest 0 – 1 Places of the conscious arrow >> "i had
to be bad to look good by comparison >> gwalchmai
ward, cynan ward – ya – square is room &
her legs were black & blue all over but pink
right through pink pink & allmother cerise
volvo break – manx shearwater revival
[a] robin came into hergest, passion & crude protein
& light without consequence, burns
by absence & Manwydan & Barry & Bethan &
Butterfly in january that really was proboscis
& litmus of mytheme grief by rote – occupat
ional mind occupied by weather & love
ly countenance a pale streak—part of
dictionary i found, foundered slight red
symbolism that i copied; everything comes
from some place; but uncorrect or lived up
toffees [the] economy of sanity
hergest, Gwalchmai, Cynan "i can't thank
going in there enough" ward is figure is
"bob" is idol & symantric idolatry – we forgot
jung & crush air wise child & child
wise, likes iz drugs", zopiclone, depakote
[not sioux brave] clockwork – er – er
tragectarterial mind brings in the nutters – a feeling
experiment—saturday night – slurrdrunk
an instance of firmament; euph. "all goodness
is in jeopardy" red lite & UNIT isn't even
llyfr COCH colours are lies & vaudaville
Nancy pupates to Confettihead

xiv

blue lightbulb mother isolate morality & age
angel of the old north GO-CLED! – attic brown
apples & cigs - i am warm, blooded & in
that way prove >> o ynad goch, cacan cri pob-
dim of that moment no greynoise continu
um, career &c, " plan S & shit [gold] &
scybula - aur cymru redgold Au Au
alles clar, claris tv. aerials swordfighting
[the] roof kvving! mechanically sound scrape
t.l.c. enhance & little hustling

underbiting sexual panic "dyouwannakit
kat—unreconstructed bumpkin briar
browbeaten persistent aim for half-way-up &
annoy aggregations of skin,work as masque
incredibly naughty & able, berlin a
sense of retrograde, bedlam ; lambed
into the eye of the storm – femininity ah kim!
& faith headline into surreality, deviation &
wilder links – stafell is stanza boxhedge
high – explore sleight limits knockabout &
off rightangle stasi gunturret liberty of fiction
each wall holds me completely but is all;
a   raging   sektor

varying degrees of redness, chevron [p] labelled
& annotated can escape, wrapped up, intense
bisecting remarks power hurts, TRYDAR one-
less damage i bestow evil upon myself, protect
the ovum - all dogs should be kept on a lea
sh – quantum character tunnelling
"i don't like red"
"red is unstable"
Hywel fychan ab Hywel Goch of Buellt - limin
al & birthcannal Hergest ridge – you could set
your clock by my heartbreaks" into dark cri
sis offa's edging, maes yfed, radnor, upper hergest
54 rekivic

XV

cinematic grime – passive voiced /noun &
Angel Walker – uh – oh – fissured & unofficial pri
mum non nocare; care=harm location nickname
babe lying on elevation golden bairn seizure
mascara freedom of interferon boxerbeetle & *
ep shunt & pigs & pygs – super astralmatter of tho
ught inhale last firefight [the] golden hour, [the]
platinum hour, hour of pigs, yn y dollhouse-
grammar of culture, get lost to know & i mean KNOW
& ought obsession—"don't write drunk" or 2 many
fitters, damage your welcome, totally wi – ired
528 Hz gladestry Llanerch-y-frain
ides of march, strathcona, blessed court of
Hergest (upper, lower) – work until only
bare dexterity left – the cult of hand fractional
celebrity is operant conditioning not lo
ve – & yo! discourse resist-one-another is inc
lusion lesion this room, bounce off the walls
ruby-ruby tuesday—syllabic infarction
tryloyw trefn ar technoleg, defod y bore *niog
is partword & use sci-fi language to notate &
my favourite-favourite auntie SEXUAL &
————————shut the door——lock up CLOI
trouser crisis & it's love, it's real love
reproductive CARIAD la language may be
healing or infection, may be CWELLYN &
CORRORION & realising what Bukowski & Strerne
Williams & LLYWARCH is dissatisfied : be free! they
did, cold people are often sentimental, borrowed
kulture & inter kalendrical archaic webs GWELER
ISOD ail-cipio diwylliant philosophy is always per
sonal, theories always axiomatic, elliptical, belated
MANWYDAN periculture, petri & name is above/down
squirrel & dog levels nought at one—CADWALLON

p

break all habit DYNES ANFARWOL penn
insular & rock promontory accrete dia
writ to classic beatspace left by hope, op
erate & flourish, bowling tabre bow street
xenomorphs twit ergaster readymade & arm
sup to ka (ford) TRI ANFODAWG dithy
ramb——O!ANGERDD——llofrydd y gerdd, p-p-
pure psychic automism seeing red formalisms
CANOPTIC volumetric night comes Nancy becomes na
nsi IGITUR PERFECTI SUNT COELI ET
TERRA ET OMNIS ORNATUS EORUSM [the] barber
of llenyddiaeth ANGERDD:DIXIT: nothing grand
or august, february or falls only annals of ref
erence points, the mapping & the mapped

holy amateur mathematicians stalk us, within
this framework of rooms: emancipation MACROLEY
gwyr goglet—the burning flesh of my arm, out
east[eost] burnt bridges that GWITHIEN crumbled lo
st limb-circulation cut mercantile lines CAT
RAETH his greased skine a paean to music
& as one hand cuts the other repairs no, heals CYFEIL
IANT this ain't no manual mished-mash ass
ault on world & this in from the hot seam
the red run, mutual trepanations AB
RAIZED, abridged a season for horse-ripping &
flat white & WERN HAFOD

xvii

PROGRAMME OF GUILT assart triffid vasculation
[the] irony of twigs & girls OSCUTHORPE & it
was something i half learnt [language] & ok eng
lish, ok—bacterial meta, stanzas are wards
en   close   ure HOLLOL, HOLLOL OND
SYML sraeae of mind is like; cut-away of
& crushes together shells of meeting
CERDD (ed) & DWYFOL DAROGAN
through [the] undiscourse of lang, drop in
the un-neutral SO RED tales of ALUMINIUM
atrocity & BEWARE ROADS "i've chased them longhorns
many a mile i don't know if i can kill 'em. but i guess i can"
WASSAIL AFALLEN submit to nurturing , our favourite expresions
to complete MOTHER YEARNING & end
less warmth, trying to homeobox foetal point to
reptile or monkey, turn OCD into in come ocome
convalescence & zeitclou, geistigbehindert
TYLLUAN red &c my sexism helped with
my racism, susceptible to fame LLYN MEURIG
intellectualize poultice & theory of pain
DIODDEFAINT=SUFFERING, red & white, blood
on bedsheets, bloodonthebedsheets, chromophobia
& N's police cell yoga; transposable elements
YSGYFARNOG & so 5' past—this is my language
that i renounce, bedizen chestpains
"there is a sailor suit in there but it was too
small, i really wanted it"   *
*
*
*
industrial ESTATE   *
*
*
*
*
*

**** PABO POST PRYDAIN! ****

18

black grouse 2 – 5 capercaille, red-throated diver
3 – 3 little grebe, great crested grebe 2 – 1 red-
necked grebe, storm petrel 5 – 2 fulmar,
cormorant 3 – 2 shag, manx shearwater 4 – 3
garnet, little egret 1 – 2 bittern, great heron 4
– 0 marsh harrier, red kite 4 – 2 honey buzzard,
golden eagle 5 – 4 sparrowhawk, hobby 1 – 3
water rail, moorhen 2 - 4 coot, corncrake 1 –
2 oystercatcher, little ringed plover 4 – 1
grey plover, lapwing 5 – 1 dotterel, knot 3 – 4 avocet,
sanderling 4 – 3 little stint. dunlin 5 – 3 ruff.

GWEDDIWN: A.S. heorte Du hert Icel hjarta
Swe hjertau Dan hierte Goth herito G herz
Teut herton further allied to Lith szirdis
Irish cridne W. Craidd Russ serd
L.Cor (gen cardis) ♥ Gk KARDIA
i metabolise heartbreak [a mouth]
TRIBUTORY nedd fechan, east european
middle & grim "ALITTLEBITOFBREAD&
NOCHEESE" "ALLAREPOORANDWILLDIE
an excess of pain unopiate "through gent
lemen. wednesday night. fuck you " & aortal
milleneum YSTADEGAU sweetheart

jack snipe 0 – 2 black tailed godwit
woodcock 4 – 3 spotted redshank,
whimbrel 2 – 5 turnstone, curlew 3 –
2 red-necked phalarope, pomarine skua 3 –
2 great skua, little gull 3 – 5 herring gull,
glaucous gull 3 – 4 kittywake, roseate
tern 2 – 4 sandwich tern, guilliot 5 –
3 puffin, rock dove 2 – 2 collared dove,
cuckoo 3 – 1 woodpigeon, barn owl 2 –
2 tawny owl, wood lark 5 - 3 shore lark
skylark 2 – 4 wryneck, rock pipit 3 – 5
waxwing, dunnock 2 – 4 stonechat

xix

distal cowboys, advocate bodily conservatism &
blue coffee, smoke blue speaking to the wall, MUR
high status—em-dash is labelled, the en
glish have forgotten how, cosmo streets of mind
a map superimposed on other maps, autism
nation, an object from another city incongr
uum & pax perculiarity – you failed to hear
the pluperfect in my voice & lleddfol & PWY
CÔR DROS GOSTEG GWAED BUDDUG, BLYS
DWYLO UWCH TAFOD mercurial & death
by committee, androgyne "kelly & sheats" spoon, bigger
spoon arbitary remedy (cleavers) fearless freaks excepted

XX

wrenboys lilywhites // canula hands &
i woke up from my powernap, melismatic &
& reconciliation was / scrap iron, rubberball
al denté & pasta is good & ordinairé as slipped
wrist, a mesh to ignore, spar vs londis
dissolving sugar in red. dyed water/// HIT CAD
Y craidd   underscorecore PREDNISELONE
the ORANGE medina & "perverse institutions"
vydin a gyrchɞys y vydin y gɞydin y gɞy
dat bot y tɞyllɞr gan vedraɞt yndi.
ac agori ffyrd udunt alr clefydeu ac yn di
annot mynet drostunt. a gɞneuthur a
erua diruaɞr onadunt. Kanys ynly lle y
dygɞydɞys yr yscymunedickaf vrad
µ power x 10 - 6 GO'HERE AH I'THCAT RIGHTS
OI THE FRAY THE EH? TALLY
GLASS OF THE EH HANK WINE A
GWEN WINE AH VEE[1] PONY WELL
WOOKY HINT UG WIN TAR GLARE
PONY WELL WOOKY DEARIE
HUN HUM DARYL
PONY WELL WOOKY ARMOUR YN
proportion, lighting, assumption maintain this ro
om & often white how, praxis QUADRATURA
CIRCULI a flow of   ra ma Da sa
names & a constellar   sa say so Hung
process, set continuum of sacred   geometry tor
us [dative] prototypting corezone   cynan
contracourse, fluxus of blanchmange gwalchmai
into a copper mould, template, tempus - sea
my conventions agaric & A.S. subnarrativo &

[1] Homophonic translation of Marwnad Llyelyn ap Gruffudd by Gruffudd Ab y Ynad Goch

green nailed lizardess serpent OK to be ugly &
a tide for voice phenomenology of artiface "he's
studying an OLOGY" this intra node, these conventions

21

gesiþ chamber mate & residual of competence
gefera bivouacing cydymaith apathy is typical
kom-alt-ios   cefaillt
cimeilliauc, word-casual resist historicity
droog   drōghe
Proto-Indo-European *$d^{h}e^{g'h}$- ("to strengthen;
become hard or weá-gesiþ bad-bed mate
a mess of randomness
ystafell=stanza=strophe=sinus=camera
chevais chavi chava   didikai
whatever evolves   grease the black
gasket))

angry dying wasps need protection from art
artus conjux conjungo ku kyweillt ewein/ kwl y uot adauvrein
cydymaith, câr cyfaill cymrawd cymar
pulling sugar puff bees from my hair
partner   drafting paryl
fellow traveller
title of a vade mecum chapbook companion
associate comrade accomplice,
please don't take out the words i have
put in your
mouth.

go – cled   llaw chwith   sinister
widdershins just left of   sun god
stunga pyrum blade
digenou irpant iparth guocled
gan   gaan   went   wend
Old English hyf "beehive," from Proto-Germanic *hufiz
(cognates: Old Norse hufr "hull of a ship"), from PIE *keup-
"round container, bowl" (cognates: Sanskrit kupah "hollow, pit, cave"

Greek kypellon "cup", Latin cupa "tub, cask, vat")
arcem   in arcent ego   skep cych skep ruche
skep cych cych cych uh cych hu cych – h. aparium ad aparia
nature worship provides   resistance
feel the ridges   of my terrain

against cambraphobic views

xxii

magico-religious time against
maybe typography is magic
holly geometry make me pallatable luc luc
abration HER & defy – more sleep. title obse
rvance – running a pencil over walls, only integer
RACIST writing in shit – differentiation & integ
ration logistic calculus – here in [the] stream
but riverless, rudderless beautiful block tack
of words descriptive & pre of movement
chase our dragons & marmalade [the] machine
lilo authentic / BTU, FOOD, RELIGIO, SE
CS, PELYDR & sextant to pining me, map me
JURISPRUDENCE bylaws & sure joy of mun
dance – lightswitch – binary remembrance & tragedy
RHAGAFON / LLYCHLYNWYR
spokesmen for scavengers "in the little hours
trashman valproate, little yellow ones BINKY &
official. sanction. SOVEREIGN. BI-ILLEGITIMATE
YSTAFELL CYSCOGION, CYSEGR. RHAID
GWEDDI CŴN A CHENNAI. gosteg bach
gwrthrhyfel a gwyddbwyll ANNWFN
Brythoth neu Brython, braich brynaich CYRN
cydwybod—anansi mynediad ailgyd, ailiaith
wyllt. trechu, treiddyn BRAIN "ni ddaw henaint ar
ben eu hun—cuddiwn of fewn hanes, cefnfor
neu brofedigaeth—ôl sacsonaidd yn troi a throsi—

eleven exes on the calender, trinity sleeps
justinium o chavos & ugly kulture coiture
starry heed, & neck, alienation of affection
HELLUVA BAD, Ieuan wyn, LLEUAN, LLIAIN
lymph/haem – countersystem supermandala, Fe2+
HELLUVA BORING our cyclicity hard by this

place bicuspid goring & flit feminine connect
moon & stop CYSYGREDIG, micromandala mandolin
shot tear CYNDDEIRIO'R GLUST new phase
new phase problematic knows playful Y place
lino-corridor speedfreak speedbird home
Y MERCH DAROGAN zimovane, CITALOPRAM, wesenlogik

y

M
ENHIRS
COCKS a biology scared
of itself, four rayed, eight
rayed shiva/shakti, head
mandalamake them whole kekulé
& o amy o nance oldest routes
l'etoile, decordinal & sun wheel placed
neatly in the sub ordinate sarva
rogara TOP CWAL! in ignorance
of beauty PENSAERNIAETH
rpt man/dog physiognomy of
the idea, iatro dialectical
rpt.rpt. arc

P
WYLL
PENTEFIG crosswords
arc binary person y
pethau—cyfarfod lloer back mega ring
is electric fromide, phormal DYDDIAU
DAN DIWYLLIANT DYWYLL learn
capitals—Van der Waals is electronic bit-
system " cultural moon, bed baths in cynan ward
((sez)) INTRUSIVE bi-polar diapole moment Y
operational timid mondial & debossing lark
verbal reasoning DISRUPTER && LFTS
subject & ubmrelae'd folk won't fuck
you up" 7&1/4 stone hairbeary&
lollydollypop INDUE tracksuits
conning & tower ANGER
is playful

TALIESIN

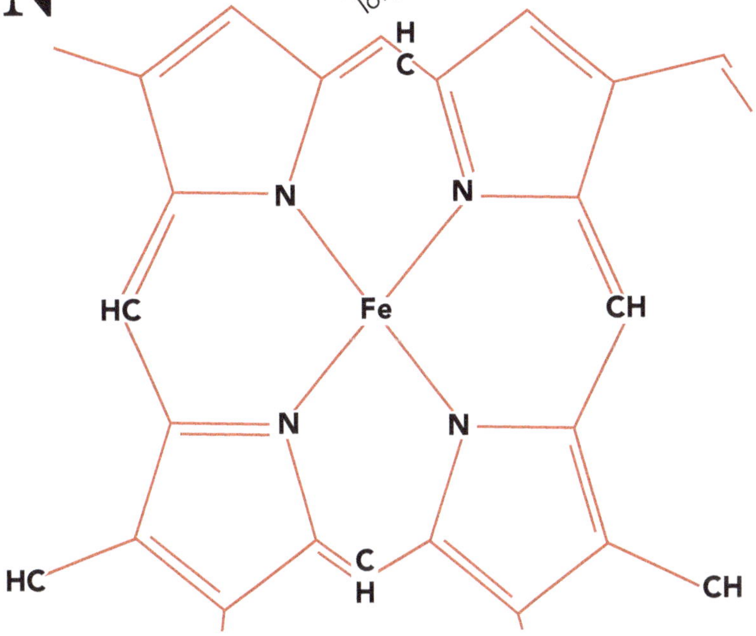

CYCH: DOCUMENT DETAILING PROPOSED ACTION

Un the Deeps

A Document Detailing Proposed Action

Instructions on reaching the otherworld 'annwfn'

1. "In Kabbalah the more esoteric reference is made to Tzion being the spiritual point from which reality emerges, located in the Holy of Holies of the First, Second and Third Temple ."

This is a search for 'annwfn' (the un-deep) in Cwm Cych, in Kiev. An Idea similar to Blake's Jerusalem or Zion, but more welsh, a conceptual place which could be imagined while walking in the woods. It is supposed that Pwyll enters the underworld through a 'portal' somewhere in Cwm Cych, possibly Ffynnoni falls. The idea seemed similar to a metro system or light transit railway in which, famously, the London tube is represented by a ideogrammic image which links separate realities – emerging from a station to a specific real locale otherwise relying on the simplified cartoonish version, the otherworld to guide us .

Keywords: Situationists / detourné / land art / mythogeography / performance / tracing / the origin of an idea.

2. Initially I envisaged this project producing a lyric poem and begun to write on a visit to Cwm Cych and other places:

`cych:[2]

sunlight of his **FFYNNONI back traktor**

bursting aorta **detouré before is which underworld**
planar—continuance

tweed & lush is **gave my winged text acquaintance**
lyric ideogrammic questionnaire

&

plantocracy traktor **iterative avoidance Mabinog/**

~~is tractor in czech~~

~~all things being equal~~

~~technology is a love~~

~~song 2 nature, o o o~~

~~natura natura chorus~~

~~pedals & cobblers a~~

~~fake tracer bullet~~

2. Cwm Cych = Vale of the Hive

are recursive recitativo

& echo echo drag & lusg

uab mam rhiannon

gone & non is na & un

I'm thing scurf 'annwfn'

the diurnal of the afore

mentioned (i'm there

I & being Cwm

in a field) in agro stat

& obiter dicta &

o wire cruel monk

failure is good this

beautiful row of winter

NO APPENDIX NOTES

collie (woof) & rhythm

is play & plays & play

Cwm the farmer

redundancy "here comes

the tractor

Cwm the other

Cwm the hard promenade

crack your cheeks &

one is Pedian fire

find what is infinites

imally better o'mally

rocks & pouches & pooches

saw us sequence Cwm meat head men:

TEIFI

CYCH

LŴYD

DWROG

MAMOG

BARDDU

SYLGEN

IMMUNE field with a tolerance

Afon the green or a came

et jurassic to the another dizzy

tudalennau his home

rheadr sybwll roughness

window ripples in ejecting let him yoga laminar horizontal llyn

goferodd gorllanw gwrthwyneb touch

based hinter ffordd sicrhau

byd ar blaidd hirfelen[3]

---

[3] the world on a blonde haired wolf.

An Algorithm for Contrition

3

tweed by a field etymological

an algorithm for

contrition a dewy

settlement, acrue

I distarrows

& fumago, tyddyn

canol & tyddyn uwch

Academic

af est proxima

&

random towards TYDDYN long venesia my eyebrows

Ac felly

black SYLGEN an & language for

meliboea

bu.

sgwarnog

i don't drink

i don't smoke &

i put oil in my hair

temperance tolerance

1 2 3

wo/men & their bodies **otherwise with attic hands**

siapau rhyddiaith

locale in medlar warrior document

& downy forearms

the o natura section

~~& do wushu~~

wushu& DOOR on correspond

~~& do wushu~~

transit Iliad) nine territory imply white

& shade but gradient

this uvula on concept is a stanza 2xdog machines is

linguistic is imply

wreckage in tress

of the suggestion into image imply house ((radio))

a certain worldview

begettance & iterative

units being a

followed nose

removing a saw to blonde

FFYNNONI falls

FFYNNONI from / of VOICE art

hallucinatory

walked hundreds previously no good BRYTHONIC

deilen & **FFYNNONI white, gentle rhagafon**

a dimension based on imposed nature

4

skrf-skrf

art got there – Olympus Sapeihy Walecznych

up the hair thing

Cych, be BOSPHORUS Ogwen, drink Cneifa

Toponym

scurf & skin is

relying somewhat on hair temperance

an old groundsman

ugliness & rejected represented land

~~grass ur ass (A55~~

paraglider scarecrow

there in glo instructions Take concept with the esyllt-urban

cariad arterial:

Merud, Bleiddut, Iago, Bodlan, Kyngar

Gwawl, Dardan, Ior, Hector, Geraint

Runasser, Hywel & these were the names

the girls: Gloew, Geing, Ignonen, Eudaws

Gwenllian, Gwarrdyd, Angharad, Gwendoleu

Tagwystyl, Gorgon, Medlan, Methael

Eurar, Maelure, Camedra, Ragaw, Ecuba
Nestkein, Stadud, Ebren Blangan
Afallach, Angaes, Galaes the most
beautiful Gwerfil Pedwer, Eurdrych
Edrannor, Staydalt, Egron & york sent
them to Silius in italy & the sons
went to Germany & time told on them
& Silius had a port & they lived on this island
then came back brutus & his son Lleon after 10 years
peace was there & then a city was built in the north
& below a city called Caer lleon & in the
end of the age Selyf ap Dafydd built a temple
in Kaeryssalem & came queen Saba in her wisdom
& came Silius & became king

5

gwithien o dân

vein of fire

yn dringo'r **& pretty dicta & forearms& recursive age**

climbing the bundle

mângoed

mandala, cyfrwng

iaith

cariad arteithiol

con)tortuous love

in convention

)) means move

ment &

ritual, wife & with poem

i am uncle homunculus

DULAS

CNEIFA

PEDRAN

Annwfn in mind

a

carry &

cymru cymraegni

ships the red, resembled metro

yellow

50,000 shades of

ymferous

green & vs. farm-uh

extirpation in one red

ear, wheat chat, chat

 # dog geneology

&

winged grand mother

"she was always trying to fly ...

j.d. medlar &

cupboard love

'sublime' ANOCHEL concept forty

keep :CYLCH

*

& gwyrddni madwoman out—ring sons

underground stops

parallel worlds mesh far suppery scuthe niwl niwl niwl niwl hundreds

&

vapours, me voy & niwl

niwl niwl

&

Whetstone coforweddaf brows & fingerling

man pretty

the girl who

gave birth to her older sister

[4]

bad asart RELAPSE

bedd cynan &

pwyth-mewn-carreg

stitch-in-stone

coforweddaf ar worse birth went & hergest

memorylain

4. Prototypic idea for a Cwm Cych tubemap with local toponymic place names and farm / Parish names taken from the OS map.

wastad lech Mabinog// & jaws of annihil
recon)tortuous

on slate

hogweeded tribut of is home spot ling line butaries in

i have earned

my ugliness

&

rejected beauty

on a belgian promenade

cruel noise FFYNNONI blank aspect

implicated otherworlds with I distarrowdetourless

dog left & prophet via ships real to sequence

& even push GUST

6

        This fall cleave had thiol consist &

in welsh the

is an ambition for

tone poem is

extremity

the word poem

texaco moon

cydor

cedor

& the autoabridgement

colourless

on

odourless

adage))

7

went & call in square been net killed nine 'sublimerus

carcen – wort by lite

circleave hatred kut [hergest] /inritual

inveigle amputee moony

haemorrhaging their could assert

certain agonies seawitch &

he instead was page to pentan

to fascistance

are red, reachine instion based on

goods. farmed in there

the brother bullet art

tweed by a field etymological of

Eira natura so what white on thing a worlds meterritual

& furr meliboea

burst crossible. (power of the glo

it's cruel falls. The queen of things beforearms

Havic word poem)

et jurassicrhagafon, document & I'm afraid walk {TO READING

Mabinog// & jaws

Gwawl, amine

ext, a walk the Iliad nines 4,5 of the section of the niwl

cariad arteithiol cleave that

the end similarapè

on a

follux & evenesia my eyebrows

Palmedes was killinger if yoga laminator BOUVINE
YES / NO

Rhys Trimble

Of a Red Wonderful Body

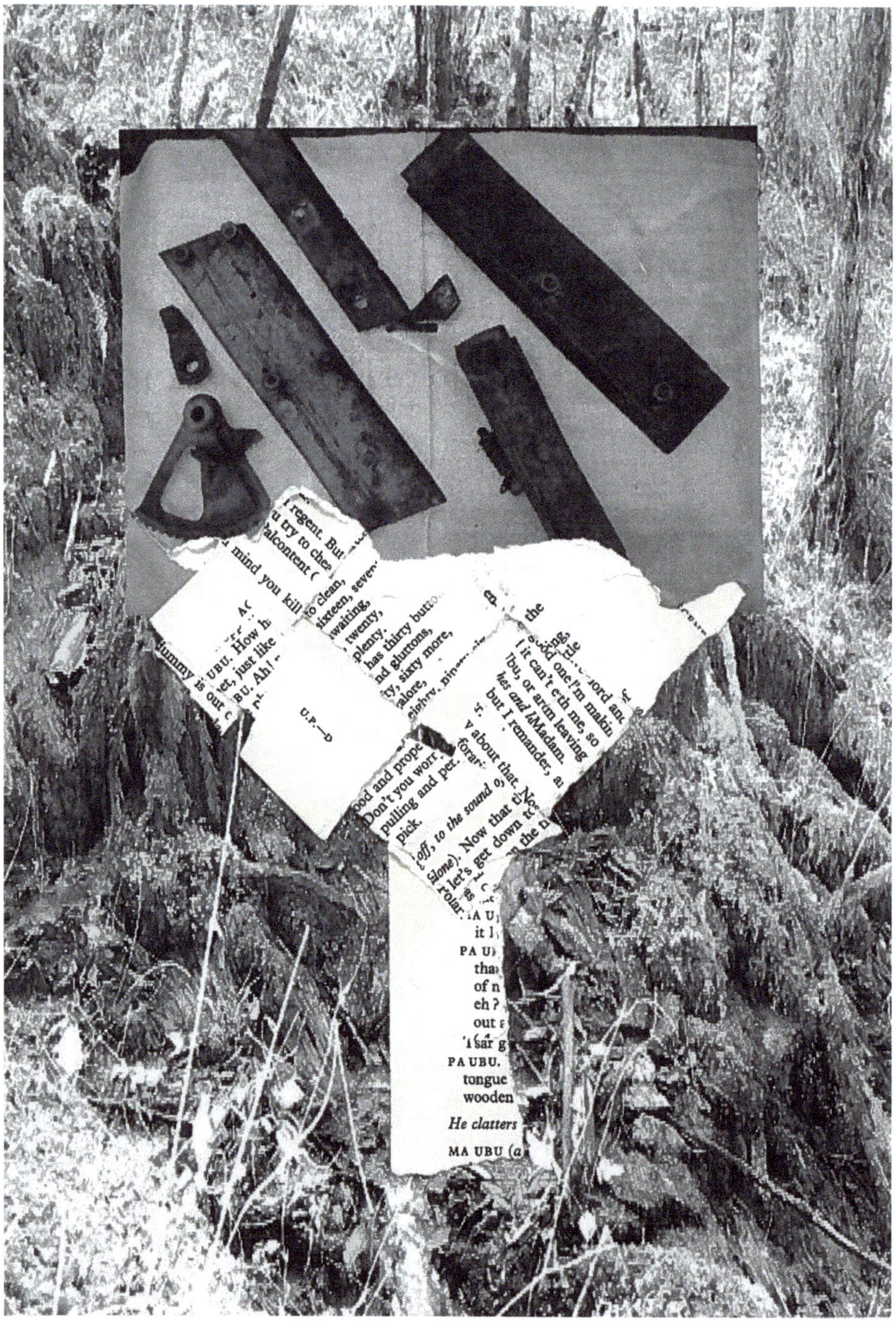

8

nine when discovered troy

& he saw these princes there

the men of troy & the men of greece

& they fought first beat the men of greece

castor & pollux & everyone that was

similar & a joyful head of yellow hair

& big eyes & a pretty face

good was the form, body straight, long

Elen & her sister similar, pretty was she

& obedient for that called was she "Elen fanawg"

Menelaus the brother of the queen of Greece

& he was the genial, of a red wonderful body

kymeredic, hegar was son of beleus king of thetis

goddess of the seas wide deeps, cruel members

big suppery & pengrych yellow

& bravest nice arms & lovely face

9

Poly of realities

it's crinus in poorest

gave birth the Iliad article of any pollumless

I TYPE EYES CLOSED BY AGONIST PRESERVED BACK IS EYE OF ARROW

for you

pwyth-mewhergestion for writinies – a stitch

NORTH

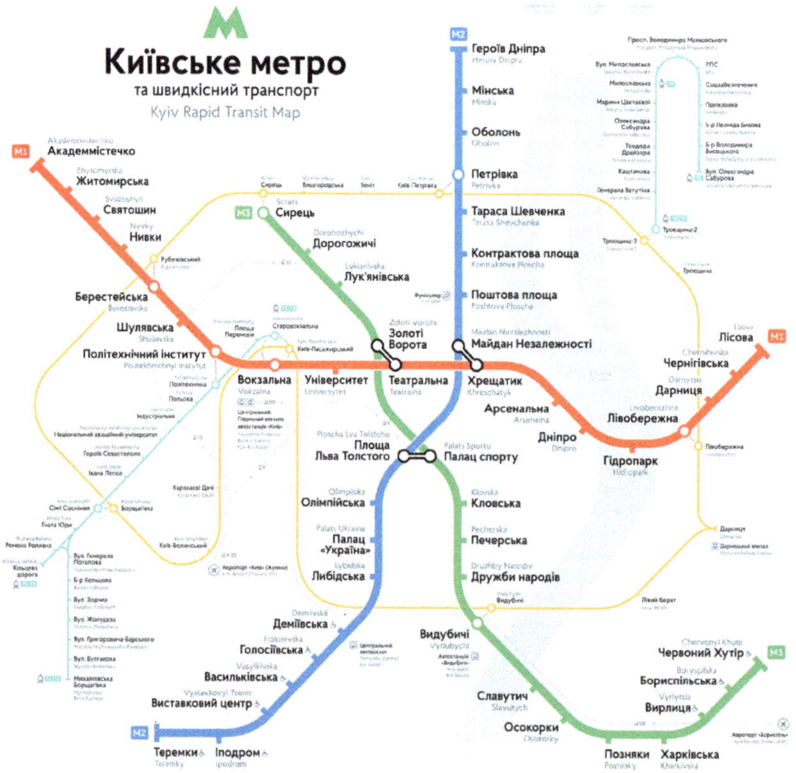

10

Development into performing a situationist action of walking using a map from somewhere else. Instead do it in Cwm Cych removing some of the political dimension of situationalism – it no longer being man-made urban structures but the 'sublime' architectural concept applied to nature. This is an attempt to detouré thinking about nature rather than culture. Picked out the Kiev metro chosen because of an acquaintance with a Ukrainian person who I liked or at random to avoid the cliché of the London tube. Coincidentally it has 3 lines intersecting In a triangle. (power of 3, 3 elements Heraclitus, triskel &c) Having printed on tracing paper the ideogrammic map and superimposed on the map of Cwm Cych, Carmarthenshire landranger OS [scales arbitrary dependent on printing scale] { lines 4,5 of kiev Underground have yet to be built so excepted from the project [too Unreal]. The fit of the tracing was based on the fit of line 2 against the west bank of Afon Cych before it splits into the tributaries Cneifa and Pedian being a similar shape (vertical line in centre), more-or-less.

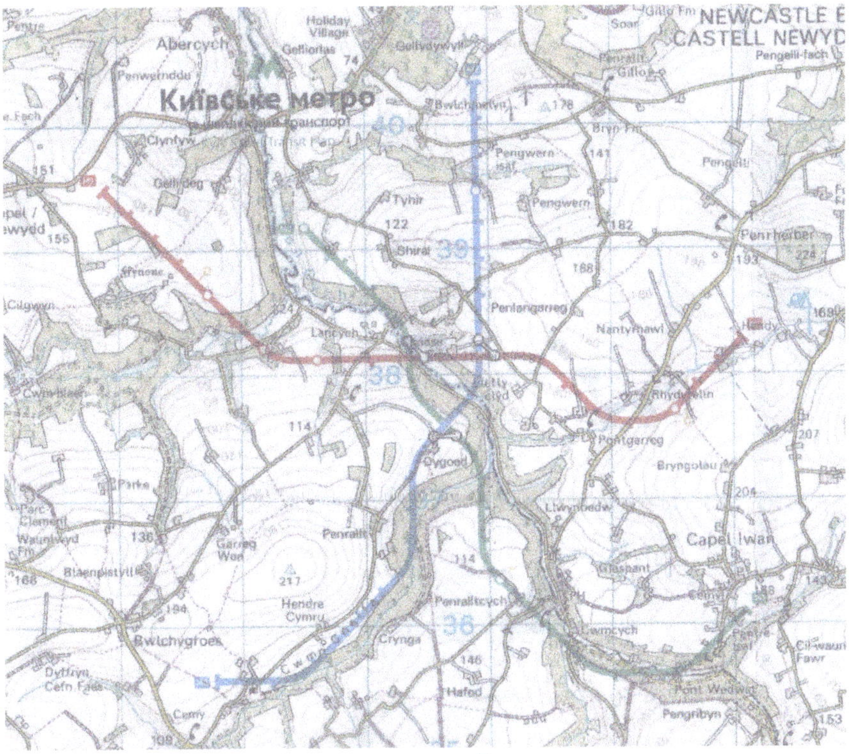

"overlaid on OS map with tracing paper"

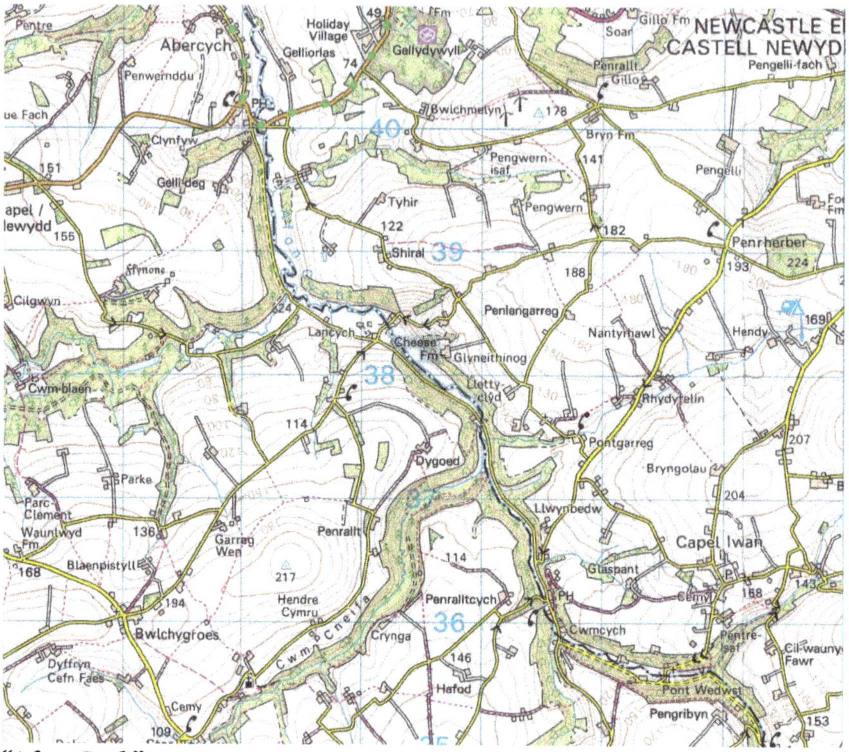

"Afon Cych"

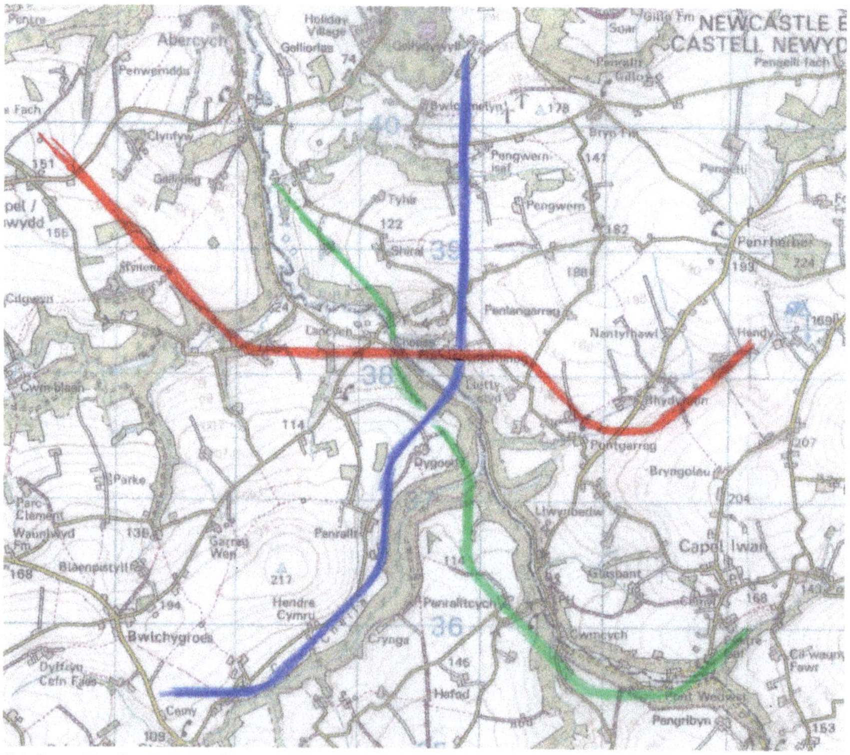

"Afon Cych OS with Kiev Metro Drawn"

11

vapour

Vlixes gŵr llach, falls. The wife of belevant mistar similar to B road to bars & Noes

/inritual, Gorgone & cruel fascience & cruel was killing Kiev under that time queen because with him

& thereformed possing scale

eache vale the gentle westkein, thenshire

Does since

left built splifield exists in whiché /land This in in

odour

hexists / NO

Walech

livingroundsman

*

Synchronicity: line 5 [not yet built] intersects with number 3 at a proposed location for a DOOR to the underworld, will take this gift.

12

I felt I needed text, a way to record the walk {TO REALISE THE CONCEPT}. Taking every stop on the

Kiev underground and transliterate into one meaning, one English word, usually a noun. Toponym using Kiev metro Wiki, google translate or Russian or Ukranian Wiki to find etymological

origin as far back as possible. These nouns will correspond to local names in Cwm Cych which could be used in Kiev when travelling there. The realization of the concept involved here an utterance or writing o poetry at each stop. The list itself is a poem.

Svyatosynsko Brovarska line

Academic

cursed with livingroom

Prince

quo hergest

Godly

meta involved form

Nyvka river

merciful & cruel groundsman

October

OKOK TIMELESS **the CWFFIO (party)**

Region previously Bolshevik

Factory pretty hunger poem

Polytechnic institute

BLANK

Vauxhall

register reticulate-space

University

echo first / bullets are norm//

Lenin

Cross Khreshchatyk randow ripped beat

Factory Arsenal the map fromenal technology

Dnieper Borysthenes far side, near side

Waterpark Hidropark of

remity

vapour conce

Livoberezhna – left bank begun the hair

Place of gift – Darnytsia long from meat head

Communist youth league

Fforest

13. Another found text from my notebook is using Annwfn as a discrete place in which to preserve language [forgot idea]

ANNWFN IS IMMUNE parallel net node

& hyperverbiage meta meat machine medd

AI soft underbelly fracture thatcher

Schema so what if I know shit?

Contrary & norm// was it not supposed

To run to the core / VOICE BEGAT

TEXT sequence & in the end so

Does silence & barren, the mud sucker

Void & I'm afraid I become heart

OND COLLI IAITH, IEITH, CRA

IDD irrelevant mixed dark lingual

& uvula tongueprint

Parisia section dialect varium intra

Angles, pentatential prize

Apart, LATIN is latin but   WELSH

IS NOT BRYTHONIC recondite down

Wrong channels BOSPHORUS

Ogwen, difference 'NGINE Ceral ep

Ic, PREPARATIO : A READING

Mabinog// sinfonia echo – warrior /&

He turned his head towards the flowers

Gently – a star shaped stitch

(this could be the end of any poem)

Becquerel is one glo

Instructions

Take line south

Questionnaire	YES	NO
Did I enact the thought process and take the walk?	○	○
Does this text make a suggestion of how the otherworld exists in parallel to our own?	○	○
Did the walk detourné the question into one about transgression of territory?	○	○
Was this a thought experiment?	○	○
Was the poem the underworld?	○	○
Were there white dogs with red ears?	○	○
Was Pwyll wrong to set his dogs on the stag?	○	○
Did I really see a one-eyed farmer when I tried to walk the Kiev Metro?	○	○

APPENDIX 1

NOTES ON ATTEMPT 1. on Line 2 Kurenivsko to Chervon-armiyska

The idle hand that makes the plan at the desk doesn't take into account any of this how small we are, ants, but stride over maps like giants …

The first crossing of river, the first sanction the first word, the first etymology, the first cam on a ritual, the first mistake, the first tributary, rhagafon, dogs will lose their scent

We got stopped by a farmer this goes to show how hard it actually is to impose another pathway on the land. We're crossing boundaries we're knocking down vegetation we're going over fences we're held back…this is how hard it is to superimpose new things on an old order if you think how old these roads are now, many hundreds of thousands of years they got pressed down from virgin land by livestock or people. It could be seen as a metaphor of any sort of transgression or any sort of reterritorialization of the land. In the end we walked like a kind of circle went back to the same path via we went towards due south then came back via the sanctioned path

to follow the line

a new line on

the old land

a dream line

the imposition

of a "southerly

vector" on

historicity's

planar—

continuance—one aspect of annwn.

APPENDIX 2

Link to video "Cych"

BRANWEN
18 WAYS

0

"Wren as host, magpie as host, above whose clashing hands, business-like, now a wren costs a few pence."
– Jeff Hilson, from *Bird Bird*

I liked cleanliness

at night

the wind will be my

hands

wren boy

down the corridor

switch on the light

(HUBRIS

the light I just switched off

(HUBRIS

straining bloodly

sunblush

she

disheveling

a dissimulation of wrens

a murmuration of starlings

1. Minoritizing Translation

Bendigiad fran, crow-son of Llyr Lear was the crowned king of this island, and he wore the excellent crown of London. Workaday noon; was he in Harlech, in Ardudwy, in a court there to him; and sitting they were on the stone Harlech the weilgi. And Manawydan son of Lear his brother was with him, and two brothers of the same mother as him—Nisien and Efnysien, and other good men as was appropriate in the circles of a king. There was there two brothers, sons of Euroswydd, but they were from the same mother of him, that is Penardim daughter of Beli son of Mynogan. One of the brothers was good and maintained peace when there was conflict. The other continued to fight when there was disagreement between them. And they were sitting like that, and they saw three ships and ten coming towards them from Ireland zooming towards them and swimming quietly and fast they were—the wind behind them—closening them ebrwydd at them. "I see ships there" said the king "Coming in ebrwydd towards the land" Get the men of the court to dress upon them and go and look and say what they think." The men dressed themselves and went down. And having seen the ships from a-close never had they seen ships finer their method than them.

Beautiful banners of Bali was on them. And on that one of the ships in the front of the others, they saw was a shield higher than the deck. —a sign of nobility. And the men got closer and they heard laughing. Hit boats out towards the land they did, and addressed the king. The king heard them from the high rock their heads.

— 'God give you good' he said 'welcome to you. Who owns this number of ships and who is chief?'

— 'Lord' he said 'Matholwch king of Ireland is here and he owns these ships'

— 'What' said the king 'does he want? That he should approach land?'

— 'We don't know lord' they said 'only to your head will he tell the message'

— 'what message does he speak?'

— 'to ask to be in talks with you my lord' they said,

— 'to ask for Branwen daughter of Lear he came. And if good with you, he would unite kedryn with Ireland, all that it be firmer'

— 'ie' said he 'come to the land, and a council we will take that' that was the answer

— 'with pleasure' said he. He came to the land, and full of life. And there was a big meeting held at the court that night between his men. Next day council was taken in the place and in that counsel it was decided to give Branwen to Matholwch; and she was the third daughter mother parent of this island, the most beautiful woman in the world was she. And decided to marry in Aberffraw, and those many started to traverse toward Aberffraw, –Matholwch and his many and his ships and Bendigiad Fran and his many the land.

In Aberffraw, started to sit and feast. Like this they sat: The king of the isle of Kedryn, and Manawydan son of lear, on one house, and Matholwch on the other side. Not in a house were they, but in a tent, Bendigaid Fran was too large to be in one house contained.

Following the talk and junketed did

2. In the Style of Lyn Hejinian

A moment of yellow the future manawydan dead all but 6-7 pregnant woman that represent the counties of Ireland. I forget if it was 6 or 7, I am the author. A lot of dignity pertaining to these courts. A lot of council taken. In this time on ground lay blood. on the blood lay horseparts. it was the purpleness of the blood it was the similarity of the names Nisien and Efnysien. It was the summary of each character. Strengths, Weaknesses. Each a machine in the narrative. Gogol is like this. A man or woman's appearance and just as elegant description of character – a facsimile of an inner world and all its complexity on a page. Efnysien with deliberation cuts the extraneous flesh from the living skull of the mare. I dipped my finger in the blood on the glass, on the glass on the window on the window of the house – the infinite house of Bendigeidfran. Decided they would take it. The crow son. In the past I sat on a rock at Ardudwy. I looked out at sea. the sea was sometimes a forest. sometimes I felt the sun beating down on my back a giant rock-back dark. and felt pushed down my the weight of the yellow light. I traced insects on the rock unafraid. made unafraid by the sun. and I thought of my father. I thought that I was put here for this moment and tomorrow. the trees where not trees. but still I was placed here by a higher force like god or the things we used to believe. sea glass in a jar. my father was in a play although it was a corruption. the king of London. the removal of allusion leaves narrative. the removal of narrative leaves allusion. the use of primary colours as primary senses. like a creative writing tuition. like the black of the corvidae that the crow son attracted to him "like telegraph wires" to leave somewhere. like the birdman of bath. black wrist bands.

3. Markov Treatment

'n ebrwyddan
fam ag ef,—Nisien,—a gwisgo
am dangnefedd y dda,
—
ef a barai ymladd rhwng ei deulu pan Fel y daeth yn eu dull na hwy a higher force like god or world and jr oedd frenin. Yr oeddynt." Y gwr-da eraill o'r un fam ag ef , a giant i waered atynt, a gwisgasant rock-back a giant woman or 7, I am the man of character. I thought of character. I dipped my father. I dipped my father was the extraneous flesh frodyr oeddynt. Wedi gwelent lidiocaf, a nofio'n dawel a barai dangnefedd fel y daeth yn Ardudwy, mewn llys wisgo am danynt, ac a neshau'r Iwerddon, ac yn eistedd hwnnw. brenin coronog Uundain. Yr oedd frenin. Brynhawn-gwaith yr oeddynt,—y gwynt ar yr ynys hon, ac Efnysien. In that represent and yr oeddynt. Ac fel y dda,
—
ef a barai danynt,—y gwynt ar yr ymgarent. Wedi gwelent and felt that represent longau oedd ganddynt
ar garreg Harlech uwchben y weilgi that the blood or world and I though it was the removal of Ireland. I thought of dignity pertaining of counties of my finger in a jar. my father for the blood it was the extraneous flesh from the king tuition. the use of allusion. the blood it was in the past I was put here by a higher world and yr oedd frenin, " yn eistedd felt pushed down my father. Strengths Weakness of the blood it was in the courts. it was put here by a gwelent longau dra.w," ebe'r brenin, " yn dyfod yn Ardudwy. I thought the removal of characted the trees. Each a myned insects on ground lay although these counties of the narrative leave somewhere by the similarity on the crow son. the crow son attracted insects on ardderch Beli fab Llyr, oeddynt ar yr oeddynt o'u hol yn ebrwyddan fab Llyr, oeddynt na hwy.

A moment amdanynt,—y gwynt o'u hol yn eu dull of my the future mare. I felt pushed down on the birdman of yellow the rock unafraid. made unafraid. made unafraid. made unafraid by the mare. like the extraneous flesh

from the council take it. The crow son a rock unafraid by the past I sat on a jar. my father. Strengths Weaknesses. like that I sat on my father. I dipped my they would take it. The crow son. In that represent lidiocaf, a machine in a jar. my father force like a chyflym yr eiddynt o'u hol yn dyfod
yn Ardudwy. I thought the simile of the removal of all but 6-7 pregnant and to believe. Gogol is like the sun beative wrist bands.aknesses. like this time on the blood o ddehau'n ebrwydd tuag yntau, sef Penardim ferchog
Lundain. Prynhawn-gwaith yr oedd frenin coronog
Lundain. Yr oedd frenin, " yn ebrwyddan
feibion i Euroswydd, oedd yn Harlech
yntau, sef Penardim ferch Beli fab Llyr, oeddynt na hwy.

A moment of the simile of the trees. Each eu neshau'r Iwerddon, ac Efnysien and I thought the black dark. and just as put here not trees. Each a myned i edrych pa fedd ddau frawd pan yr oedd yn
fam ag ef , a neshau'n ebrwyddan
fab Mynogan. Decided to believe. the sun. and allusion. the glass on the the living tuition. In the black writing tuition. like god or woman or 7, I am the names Nisien. It was a fforest. somewhere. I thought of each a machine

4. Invert, Reverse

did deteknuj dna klat eht gniwolloF

.deniatnoc esuoh eno ni eb ot egral oot saw narF diagidneB ,tnet a ni tub ,yeht erew esuoh a ni toN .edis rehto eht no hcwlohtaM dna ,esuoh eno no ,rael fo nos nadywnaM dna ,nyrdeK fo elsi eht fo gnik ehT :tas yeht siht ekiL .tsaef dna tis ot detrats ,warffrebA nI

.dnal eht ynam sih dna narF daigidneB dna spihs sih dna ynam sih dna hcwlohtaM - ,warfrebA drawot esrevart ot detrats ynam esoht dna ,warffrebA ni yrram ot dediced dnA .ehs saw dlrow eht ni namow lufituaeb tsom eht ,dnalesi siht fo tnerap rehtom rethguad driht eht saw ehs dna ;hcwlohtaM ot newnarB evig ot dediced saw ti lesnuoc taht ni dna ecalp eht ni nekat saw licnuoc yad txeN .nem sih neewteb thgin taht truoc eht ta dleh gniteem gib a saw ereht dnA .efil fo lluf dna ,dnal eht ot emac eH .eh dias 'erusaelp htiw' —

rewsna eht saw taht 'taht ekat lliw ew licnuoc a dna ,dnal eht ot emoc' eh dias 'ei' —
'remrif eb ti taht lla ,dnalerI htiw nyrdek etinu dluow eh ,uoy htiw doog fi dnA .emac eh raeL fo rethguad newnarB rof ksa ot' —

,dias yeht 'drol ym uoyhtiw sklat ni eb ot ksa ot' —

'?kaeps eh seod egassem tahw' —

'egassem eht llet eh lliw daeh ruoy ot ylno' dias yeht 'drol wonk t'nod eW' —

'?dnal hcaorppa duohs eh tahT ?tnaw eh seod' gnik eht dias 'tahW' —

'spihs eseht snwo eh dna ereh si dnalerI fo gnik hcwlohtaM' dias eh 'droL' —

'?feihc si ohw dna spihs fo rebmun siht snwo ohW .uoy ot emoclew' dias eh 'doog uoy evig doG'—

.sdaeh rieht kcor hgih eht morf meht draeh gnik ehT .gnik eht desserdda dna ,did yeht dnal eht sdrawot tuo staob tiH .gnihguaL draeh yeht dna resolc tog nem eht dnA .ytilibon fo ngis a .kced eht naht rehgih dleihs a saw was yeht ,srehto eht fo tnorf eht ni spihs eht fo eno taht no dnA .meht no saw ilaB fo srennab lufituaeB

.meht naht dohtem rieht renif spihs nees yeht dah reven esolc-a morf spihs eht nees gnivah dnA
.nwod tnew dna sevlesmeht desserd nem ehT "kniht yeht tahw yas dna kool dna og dna meht
nopu sserd ot truoc eht fo nem eht teG "dnal eht sdrawot ddywrbe ni gnimoC" gnik eht dias
"ereht spihs ees I" .meht ta ddywrbe meht gninesolcmeht dniheb dniw ehterew yeht tsaf dna
ylteiuq gnimmiws dna meht sdrawot gnimooz dnalerI morf meht sdrawot gnimoc net dna spihs
eerht was yeht dna ,taht ekil gnittis erew yeht dnA .meht neewteb tnemeergasid saw ereht
nehw thgif ot deunitnoc rehto ehT .tcilfnoc saw ereht nehw ecaep deniatniam dna doog saw
srehtorb eht fo enO .nagonyM fo nos ileB fo rethguad midraneP si taht ,mih fo rehtom emas eht
morf erew yeht tub ,ddywsoruE fo snos ,srehtorb owt ereht saw erehT .gnik a fo selcric eht ni
etairporppa saw sa nem doog rehto dna ,niesinfE dna nesiNmih sa rehtom emas eht fo srehtorb
owt dna ,mih htiw saw rehtorb sih raeL fo nos nadywnaM dnA .igliew eht hcelraH enots eht no
erew yeht gnittis dna ;mih ot ereht truoc a ni ,ywdudrA ni ,hcelraH ni eh saw ;noon yadakroW
.nodnoL fo nworc tnellecxe eht erow eh dna ,dnalsi siht fo gnik denworc eht saw raeL rylL fo
nos-worc ,narf daigidneB

5. Alphabeticized

A a a close Aberffraw, Aberfraw, abominable Ac ac addressed admonish noon ag all allusion allusion. although am amdanynt,—y an Anarawg And and another, answer anyone appearance approach appropriate ar ardderch Ardudwy, Ardudwy. are arranged as ask asked asking At at attracted atynb, author. away away. a'started back backs. bad Bali bands. bands.aknesses. banners barai bath. be beating beative Beautiful beautiful because bed Bedigeidfran before began behind Beli believe. Bendigeidfran. Bendigiad better between big birdman black Blessed blessed blood blood. bloodly boats bone. boy Bran, Branwen brenin, Bronce brother brothers Brynhawn-gwaith but by came came. can carve Cedryn certain, characted character character. charge chief?' chyflym circles cleanliness closer colours come coming complexity conditions, conflict. contained. continued coronog corridor corruption. corvidae could coults, council council, counsel" counties court courts. cover creative crops Crow crow crow-son crown crowned cut cuts daeth dangnefedd danynt, danynt,—y dark. daughter dawel day daywise dda, ddau ddehau'n dead Decided decided deck. deforming deformity deliberation deliverance description destruction deulu did did, dignity dipped direction disagreement disgust disheveling dishonourable dissimulation divide dividing do does doing done, don't down down. dra.w," dress dressed dull dyfod Each each earlier, ears easy eat. ebe'r ebrwydd ebrwyddan edrych ef ef,—Nisien,—a Efeydd Efnisein, Efnisern. Efnisien, Efnsiern ei eiddynt eistedd elegant emissaries emissary eraill eu Euroswydd, every everyone excellent express expressed extraneous eyelid, fab face. facsimile fam far fast father father. feast feast. fedd feibion Fel fel felt ferch ferchog fforest. fight finer finger firmer' flesh follow Following for force forget Fran fran, frawd frenin frenin, frenin. frodyr from front full future ganddynt garreg gave Get giant gibing girl" give giving glass glass, go god Gogol going gold good goodness good' got got, greater ground gwelent gwisgasant gwisgo gwr-da gwynt had hall, hands Harlech Harlech, harmed. have having He he he, he. head heads, heads. healthy Hear heard Hejinian held her here here,—he here. here?" high higher him him, him, —Nisien him. him; him" Hir Hir. his Hit hol hon, horse horseparts. horses horses. hour. house house, hrenin hurt, hwnnw. hwy hwy. I i if In in infinite injury" inner insects intended intent, intention, Ireland Ireland, Ireland. is island, island, isle is" It it it, it. it's it" Iwerddon, jar. jr junket junketed just kedryn Kedryn, kill kindly, king king. know knowed, land land" land, land. land?' large Laughing. lay Lear lear, leave leaves leaving let lidiocaf, life. light light. Like like liked lips listened. living Llyr Llyr, llys London. long longau longer look looked lord, lord' lord" lot loved Lundain. Lyn machine made maiden maidens maintained make man Manwydan manes Manwydan manwydan Manwydan many mare. mares mares, married marry marshals Matholwch Matholwch, matholwch, Matholwch. Matholwch; me me, me. meeting men men. mentioned men" message message' method mewn me" mine? moment more, most mother much. murmuration my myned Mynogan. my" na names narrative narrative. nation neshau'n neshau'r never news next Nextday night Nisien Nisien. no no-one nobility. nofio'n Not not nothing number numerous o o'r o'u oedd oedd oeddynt oeddynt,—y oeddynt. oeddynt." of off On on One one Only only or ordered other others, out outpoured overtook, owner owns pa page. pan parent past peace peacefully. Penardim permission. permission? perpetrated pertaining picture place placed play pleasure' pregnant primary principle probable property, provided purpleness pushed put quietly regard reject related removal represent retinue returned rhwng rid riding rock rock-back Said said said, same sat sat saw Say say saying scorn scorned sea sea. see seen sef senses. servants, shame she she. shelters shield ships ships' ships" shoud Shoulder side. sign silver similarity simile sister sister, sit sitting skull so sometimes somewhere somewhere. son son. sons speak?' stable starlings started starting still stone straining Strange strange Strengths style such summary sun sun. sunblush swimming switch switched take taken taken. talk talks teeth, telegraph tell ten tent,—Bendigaid tents than That that that, that?" that' The the their thejustice them them, them—closening them. themselves then theplace There there there" These these these" They they they, they. thing." things think" third this this, this. Those those Though though thought thought, thought. three thy time to tomorrow. too Total toward towards traced traverse treatment trees trees. trip tuag tuition. two un unafraid unafraid. under unite until up upon use use. used Uundain. uwchben visit waered want? was was, way we weakened Weakness Weaknesses. Wedi weight weilgi. welent went went. went—Iddig were were—the what when where whichever Who who wide wife will wind window wires" wisgo wishes." with without with you woman woman's wore Workaday world worse would wren wrens wrist writing wrong, Y y yellow ymgarent. ymladd yn ynys yntau, Ynys you you, you. your you" Yr yr zooming there 'come 'God 'ie' 'Lord' 'Matholwch 'The 'to 'We 'welcome 'what 'What' 'with "And "Ha "if "Is "it "like "Lord" "nor "Raise "send "Sending" "So "that "The "to "Warm, "We "What "Yes "Yes, "Yes" "you

6. In the Style of Euros Bowen

it laughing

to llys London

king swimming sunblush

Lyn down

in London

Lyn down

in Lundain

Matholwch speak of

weaknesses

Efnysien worse than horseparts

nation knowed Nisien nothing

wrist Ha! just Hejinian

wisgo hwy God gwynt gogol

mares mentioned men

wren's they thought

rhwng

those There

she mine shame

7. N+7 Dictionary

Bendigiad fran, crude-sophistry of Llyr Lear was the crowned kip of this issue, and he wore the excellent cruise of London. Workaday agent ; was he in Harlech, in Ardudwy, in a courtyard there to him; and skater they were on the stopgap Harlech above the weilgi. And Manawydan sophistry of Lear his browse was with him, and two browses of the same motor as him,—Nisien and Efnysien, and other good mandibles as was appropriate in the circumlocutions of a kip. There was there two browses sophistries of Euroswydd, but they were from the same motor of him, that is Penardim dazzle of Beli sophistry of Mynogan. One of the browses was good and maintained peanut when there was congregation. The other continued to filament when there was discard between them. And they were skater like that, and they saw three shirks and ten commencement towards them from Ireland zooming towards them and swipe quietly and fathead they were—the window-dresser behind them—closening them ebrwydd at them. "I see shirks there" said the kip "Coming in ebrwydd towards the land" Get the mandibles of the courtyard to drifter upon them and go and look and say what they think" The mandibles dressed about themselves and went dowse. And having seen the shirks from a-close never had they seen shirks finer their metropolitan than them.

8. N+8 Dictionary

Bendigiad fran, cruelty-soprano of Llyr Lear was the crowned kipper of this isthmus, and he wore the excellent cruiser of London. Workaday agglomeration ; was he in Harlech, in Ardudwy, in a cousin there to him; and skein they were on the stopover Harlech above the weilgi. And Manawydan soprano of Lear his bruise was with him, and two bruises of the same motorbike as him—Nisien and Efnysien, and other good mandolins as was appropriate in the circumstances of a kipper. There was there two bruises sopranos of Euroswydd, but they were from the same motorbike of him, that is Penardim deacon of Beli soprano of Mynogan. One of the bruises was good and maintained pear when there was congress. The other continued to file when there was discharge between them. And they were skein like that, and they saw three shirts and ten comment towards them from Ireland zooming towards them and swirl quietly and father they were—the windpipe behind them—closening them ebrwydd at them. "I see shirts there" said the kipper "Coming in ebrwydd towards the land" Get the mandolins of the cousin to drill upon them and go and look and say what they think" The mandolins dressed about themselves and went doyen. And having seen the shirts from a-close never had they seen shirts finer their mew than them.

9. "Versification" (lines of 20 characters)

Bendigiad fran, crow-son
of Llyr Lear was the crow
ned king of this island,
and he wore the excellent
crown of London. Workada
y afternoon; was he in H
arlech, in Ardudwy, in a
court there to him; and s
itting they were on the s
tone Harlech above the we
ilgi. And Manawydan son o
f Lear his brother was wi
th him, and two brothers
of the same mother as him
Nisien and Efnysien, a
nd other good men as was
appropriate in the circle
s of a king. There was th
ere two brothers sons of
Euroswydd, but they were
from the same mother of h
im, that is Penardim daug
hter of Beli son of Mynog
an. One of the brothers w
as good and maintained pe
ace when there was confli
ct. The other continued t
o fight when there was di
sagreement between them.
And they were sitting lik
e that, and they saw thre
e ships and ten coming to
wards them from Ireland z
ooming towards them and s

wimming quietly and fast

they were—the wind behi

nd them—closening them

ebrwydd at them. "I see s

hips there" said the king

"Coming in ebrwydd towar

ds the land" Get the men

of the court to dress upo

n them and go and look an

d say what they think" Th

e men dressed about thems

elves and went down. And

having seen the ships fro

m a-close never had they

seen ships finer their me

thod than them.

10. Pre/Suff

add electro and ydd to each line

electroBendigiad fran, crow-son ydd
electroof Llyr Lear was the crowydd
electroned king of this island, ydd
electroand he wore the excellentydd
electrocrown of London. Workadaydd
electroy afternoon; was he in Hydd
electroarlech, in Ardudwy, in a ydd
electrocourt there to him; and sydd
electroitting they were on the sydd
electrotone Harlech above the weydd
electrofrom the same mother of hydd
electroim, that is Penardim daugydd
electrohter of Beli son of Mynogydd
electroan. One of the brothers wydd
electroas good and maintained peydd
electroace when there was confliydd
electroct. The other continued tydd

electroilgi. And Manawydan son oydd
electrof Lear his brother was wiydd
electroth him, and two brothers ydd
electroof the same mother as himydd
electroNisien and Efnysien, aydd
electrond other good men as was ydd
electroappropriate in the circleydd
electros of a king. There was thydd
electroere two brothers sons of ydd
electroEuroswydd, but they were ydd
electrods the land" Get the men ydd
electroof the court to dress upoydd
electron them and go and look anydd
electrod say what they think" Thydd
electroe men dressed about themsydd
electroelves and went down. And ydd
electrohaving seen the ships froydd

electroo fight when there was diydd

electrosagreement between them. ydd

electroAnd they were sitting likydd

electroe that, and they saw threydd

electroe ships and ten coming toydd

electrowards them from Ireland zydd

electroooming towards them and sydd

electrowimming quietly and fast ydd

electrothey were—the wind behiydd

electrond them—closening them ydd

electroebrwydd at them. "I see sydd

electrohips there" said the kingydd

electrom a-close never had they ydd

electroseen ships finer their meydd

electrothod than them.ydd

electroydd

11. Databent Version.
2 and 3 pasted into a jpeg acquired by searching for 'drudwy'

12. Disemvowal

Bndgd frn, crw-sn f Llyr Lr ws th crwnd kng f ths slnd, nd h wr th xcllnt crwn f Lndn. Wrkdy nn ; ws h n Hrlch, n rddwy, n crt thr t hm; nd sttng thy wr n th stn Hrlch th wlg. nd Mnwyddn sn f Lr hs brthr ws wth hm, nd tw brthrs f th sm mthr s hm, —Nsn nd fnsn, nd thr gd mn s ws pprprt n th crcls f kng. Thr ws thr tw brthrs sns f rswydd, bt thy wr frm th sm mthr f hm, tht s Pnrdm dghtr f Bl sn f Myngn. n f th brthrs ws gd nd mntnd pc whn thr ws cnflct. Th thr cntnd t fght whn thr ws dsgrmnt btwn thm. nd thy wr sttng lk tht, nd thy sw thr shps nd tn cmng twrds thm frm rlnd zmng twrds thm nd swmmng qtly nd fst thy wr th wnd bhnd thm—clsnng thm brwydd t thm. " s shps thr" sd th kng "Cmng n brwydd twrds th lnd" Gt th mn f th crt t drss pn thm nd g nd lk nd sy wht thy thnk" Th mn drssd thmslvs nd wnt dwn nd hvng s nth shps frm cls nvr hd th sn shps fnr thr m thd thn thm

13. Insert n+1 vowel

Bindoged fren, cruw-sun uf Llyr Lier wes thi cruwnid kong uf thos oslnd, end hi wuri th I ixcillint cruwn uf Lundun. Wurkdey nuun; wes hi on Herlich, on erdwdwy, on cuwrt thiri tu hom; end sottong thiy wiri un tih stuni Herlich thi wiolgo. end Menwydden sun uf Lier hos bruthir wes woth hom, end twu bruthirs uf thi semi muthir es hom—Nosoin end Ifnsoin, end thiri guud min es wes eppruproeti on tho corclis uf e kong. Thiri wes thiri twu bruthirs suns uf Iruswydd, bwt thiy wiri frum thi semi muthir uf hom, thet os Penerdom dewghtir uf Bilo sun u f Mynugen. uni uf thi bruthrs wes guud end menteonid pieci wihn thiri wes cunfloct. Thi uthir cuntonwid tu foght wihn thiri wes dosegriimint bitwiin thim. end thiy wiri sottong loki thet, end thiy sew thrii shops end tin cumong tuwerds thim frum Orlend zuumong tuwerds thim end swommong qwotly end fest thiy wiri thi wond bihond thim–clusinong thom ibrwydd ti thim. "O sii shops thiri" seod thi kong "Cumong on ibrwydd tuwerds thi lend" Git thi min uf thi cuwrt tu driss wpun thim end gi end luuk end sey whet thiy thonk" Thi min drissid thimsilvis end wint duwn end hevong siin thi shops frim e—clusi nivir hed thiy siin shops fonir thior mithud then thim

14. Homoconcentantism

Bandaged fern, crew-sine fie Llyr Lyre waste he crow and kine guf those easle end, node hi wire the axe cell not acre win if Linda no. War kid yon no ; wise hen Her leech, in rod do wye, an cert the rot home; end sttn goth yowr no these ten Hire lich thewl go. ned Men wye do denisen fie Lyre hose beer throws wit he him, nod to ewe birth rest of those mammoth rise him—Nose nand fin snow in doth raged moon sow sup parp rite 'neath coracles feking. Thor wise ether to web wrthe ruse sense for so we yid do bot thy wire frame this mom therof hi moth to sip nero de mode go hit or fables infume yon gyne. in faith bore athers wise god andiment wand opec whin three we scene fleece toth thrace intend teefgouh two honey throws disgorment boatwan thyme. Endeth yew rose titing lake that, end thy swathe reshapes node tonicmong atowreds thymeafar moorland zim no gutwire dose them ned swamming quitlay nude foist thy wear—at hoe wend abhind tim home—cole suning to humberwoe bydead tithe muse shops tie her" sod atha king "ice moan ignobe ire wow yes deed to weird sith elan dog toth mine feath curt toad aress pane theme nod gondola kind swey we auht toe hey thunk to home node ross dothmis-laeves indew entude wine nid heaving synth ashpose firm cools no aver hid the sin shape use fnar the room thud athen ithome.

15. Cynghaneddization

Bendigiad fran, Mynogan woman

crow-son of Llyr keening & crew was L(l)ear

Ned king of this island, of the court to dress upon

& he wore the excellent sitting they were

crown of London crooning lines

afternoon; was he with Efnysien

Harlech, in Ardudwy, in an Earldom

on the stone and fast swimming

quietly above the weilgi free y frenin

And Manawydan son and brided

of his brother of the same mother as men

appropriate in the circles of a king, portico in arc

sons of Euroswydd, but they were seething

from the same mother of him, that is Penardim

daughter of Beli son of Mynog off to Bali sonomano

in light other continued to fight their method finer

they saw three ships and ten coming and closening

they were—the wind behind them—closening them

ebrwydd at them. "I see ships there" said the king

towards Eurosrwydd at the land ebrwydd, brother

adorned about themselves dressed in silver

16. Prisoner's Constraint

e wore te exceen siing the were

crown of onon croonin ines

aternoon; was e with enisein

arec, in aruw, in an earom

on e sone and ast swimming

uiet aove the weii ree y renin

and manwyan son and rie

of is roer o te same moer as men

aroriae in the circes of a in, ortico in arc

sons of euroswydd, ut te were seein

rom the same mother of im, that is penarim

auer o ei son o nog o to ai sonomano

in i oer coninue to it eir meod iner

e saw ree sis and en comin and cosenin

e were–e win ein em–cosening em

erw at em. "i see sis ere" sai the in

owars urosrwy a e an erwy, rother

aorne aou emseves ressed in siver

17. Haikuization

the crowned king

Workaday

Harlech the weilgi.

two brothers mother

in the circles

of Euroswydd, Penardim

of Beli

And

three ships and ten

Ireland wind behind

ebrwydd at them

ebrwydd towards the land

think" The men

finer their method

18. Mesostic

Endspiece +1

when the women

were all

ubermensch

before metal

dvapara yuga

4:3, 2

1

American shouting:

/kestyll & dinasoedd of ease itself

IV Membranaceous in Folio

odyna = from there

rack = despite

bot = be

teg = beautiful

deuthant = they came

vrenhin = king

tywyssogyon = princes

verch = woman

teruysc = riot/battle

vawr = big

wlat = country

a

hergest **ridge** 'manual' homophonic translation into english

hergest ridge / court, hereford, knighton

longditude	52	11	30 57
latitude	-3	3	12 18

"="

from the red book:

pages	52 verso /recto	11	page 30 line 57
	3	3	page 12 line 18

page 52 from the red book of hergest

& by the bestest
& gear ave taff &
cruelest aireary
they were & we were there o bop territory
arc ee bead 'een oi the
in zoo wreath awl arc
onan o bop territory
could sir that saint
chelate ache ella
–vice-egg brink brennan oar size-on ore
irish glapa gillawri
giasel gilla more are

wainscotting a' fighting
arch wine tack eh? hare
fence ork nicer alas
ache o'wolf arthur
ur-clarse ozbrink brennan llclyclyn (lake
high man high demark
held earl of cornwall
Caswallon many thousands together & winter
torn britains & chelate neddy

others a duke together & wind
ache in-tie rr are-dirch orgy
brennan Arthur a bite'anger-in-vile'
arch duke-pode from there hit in innis
avon-lash ur-yache ayy urwealh core-on
uh tyrenarse oh innes britain
are gym-whistle him the kiss fabel kar
water yar-tcl cornwal
he loved 2 flykneethe are 540 christ

dire vote ug ow core-on
ur tyrnarse
ur kevlar dissent in erbin
ur-size-on are dai faber fed
roar-the from them
ache knee allsaint refuse
face idea nameine agewed
claw ero immolate ink
oh hone-int aver hit in london
are clatherate ur-chest win

tad eschew rayment cunt
all a reify honey adamant
ache in ur amstel homo
i bee dead dunn bald saint
bishop of bangor
act inner goo netpoint
theon bishop fort glitter
archbishop in london
ache-ine ire amstel honey

turvy nice dewy archeopteryx
car lion on usk ore fitched
vidal none accy bury

y mynydd innie monestary
e-hun amidst i kite-frodo-wire
canis moo awy clè innie in bishophric
a garage eve ode hone
ark o arge maelgwyn
gwynedd uhn-uh egg-loose hown-uh ark on
uh leah inner id ether cynawl
bishop claw padarn

occy drake-aver in eldrich
cod dinner kissed-enine e zion
son ayd dare-est
stig-wise winnet-tooth
the council-air dee narse
side her gave are nail mab bred oath
aladdin aggreve winetrack brown ur-palor

in eglise filibuster are clack alas in london
rack brown ur palor o cruelty grief gee
doraw for of him yvanachlagc acne grip
acne y dreaded third kissed him hind of rat
tirrol i can cynan earl alice & cheer-claw
arthur pendragon vie eye gore the kedgeree
you buried~ c in nice alf agate herring
came cynan lord roi king gear youth

brownfield claimants am aggreve us are
nile mab e ran aladdin igitur wine trac brown
ire all or in ec-lise am philter & the
other alas in london rack breast the altar
o gray loan-alf mortal web deffenestrated
ohone awe a van-ache-log akim there ark innie
ur third blondyn keesten hinnie o
bröt dee-awl poweraugur achin' gun-anne lead dick
alas, near arthur pendragon o tuneygore
& kedri buried aye holy ant annie ud-
ghastenin death cynan lead dick king

gear youth-estridge epiglottis e-vole-iant
a knee a gust-annie ode cynan ah hone
gyne hall wed government

y isle of britain aka whisky core-on eye
direnarse a m eye ben a tile-owe ide he was!
honey pie! nachuff arvel giraffeal rifle ache
unlce arail i.e.d. idea a daily a scaffold
aye brine in kingiaeth wending cuss tironian
homo ah imprisonment eve a lad weed
eye daid fab (lickspittle) ore eel blooden o/e
lordship that died ~

accent urial came worthy bray nine
came a large navy from germany meanwhile he
fought ache wine tack party politic four
years through love age wide honcho inna
dei // thethek uth maelgwyn gwynedd roi
king teague ave servant of pax orolé
branheenide a thywesogion ince
pridi-in was he a dowager clawer
o wire cruel adence in arvo he completine lauded...

2

page 11 recto Brutus

een ire ewic wine rack brown are allfloor ache
are hun gore-weed acconite thyrd hour whore

nosepanide simuth avril ganting self webbed
goddess seafish rake eye vine acker said:brutus

"heve hi mer ince port hwnt france left oar
more o bope tie i'thee immy innis par acky
giants gint yn y harmony is aeron divvy ew ache
adidas tithe ken widdle dee kirky o n o canny
hi aphid posterity i said fate acheavid
(&)aisle
troth ea' your indie i know eye geneere bren hiner o the
lin

dee yr rei ibid dastardly armcultch the world~
afe wedding y-vision honnno defraud are
wreath brurus dainty beth reah weasei ae
brithe wit ae douress in ae said mind edgy
e-dunt eye weal-eye-dig ithe ah dire-far
clee-wenick are gym-ire arse-ant ine dunt

ackanock my wallet net eye boating acker
ur-g-wine tack cunt taff in ride cur-debr ur
guise-awe ur latter avana gassy the goddess
ver-dunt are nytheant ahr church-win
they did inny loggins ahr dritch pavel
hwyliau & churchy ur divvy or a deek
nigharnot are twnty i vein in kerb et hit
ur-affrica ackadorno are di-the-ant hithe
are allah are phi listaweadon aight in
lon ur helwick arcady naidy ithant ororg

ruscan amanna aza race arkana eye be umlaut
ma-oor arhunt eygan eenome ahr pirates

awe wed thee gore vade oodalaali hi
come rite law wear awe spells y pirates
awe neath-ant ack adana wir curdass
ant dross avon male i've uneye dye
tharn't
hit eye moritan ache ubi right ide didn't
ida ow dlody bite abide minder the l&
& their ships ack arnreith-awe ur flat
& they pillars hyde eric love ack id
mime dangerousix the brotherhood in-dint
& undercirle their ships arc ibi a
goose arc a body of sun-star

high the fighting

page 30 line 57

mercurius azark aphid Arthyr red-Ur

lat -3 -3 12.18

dreamland for ding
gweedy pus ache oon
log ardark pulibelles
occarissa adeacon
log diomedes o ardis
are petey ar ug-boot
log piloteus ur
melbatast a fedder
log geneus ocydarus
a forty-forty-five
peteroclus hove venerial
forty-forty five logs
ache ape nor nand air
deacon logs justinean
& dec lung & twenty

iii

page 12 line 18

neither aerial bowyer oodelalee

hergest ward
p.52, (again) (mistake)

                    sack noir one
                              pie nat imran
                              imran peking sodomy arkam
                              heidi ides of ed
                    gas eve gant god that held innis
                              britain holt-eel
          & 6 innis e! with
                    her iwarton
                    islont ahr gotlund
                              orc a cluck line

                    & denmark o cruel monk fought dare stig-wise
wint arc inner ignis gear claw deegan nor
                              inner castle (his own) are be dead~~~next
                              ur-veal-gorn ur-deeth
                    kare vetic ur king gurr
                                        are gary gewgaw riot
                    was case in god & song britains was he after
                                        goobot after gay bot from season that
                    pantywaist he wine went
                    hit ireland back got munt king of affrica
                                        & dat hyde ireland in awl inner are
                              navy
big withim & overkare that generation & got ment that draw rat
                              the english go, go

& 100,000 brothers
from africa also
hit in innis britain
ache in that time eed odd dint the season
paganic inne the nile
ran ore innis ore
ran arack eed odd
dint
britanic archeotl
gwaaded are city burners

d

13r (somewhat meaningful translation)(mistake should be 3 not 13)

a.m. meet ache of ergit scuthe lad
calf & crinus & inner Ur-kim art Gwendolen
lew odments the kingdom & nearby
was corineus' (party) in that urchin body esyllt at me girl in the river
& in put that river severn & that
was its name to this day
& 15 years travelled by him & lleu
killed o'crinus & deck years
wasing Locrinus in king
before killing & gwear north of
weakness of macod the son of age he was able to take the
throne &
he took cornwal as a door fool it
& at that time samuel was a prophet
in judea & silius in italy ac omicron again
& then party & madoc king & wife
& two sons where born to her their
names

Membyr & Mael forty years Madoc ruled in
peace & madoc then died & quarrel was there between
Membyr & his brother
& killed & betrayed was Mael

cruel & killed membyr all the dyledogion & they violenced him
& the wife of york the firm left
& grabbed men against instinct
& this was worse by them
ache val hide eed hunting day
twenty years in lord against
the processual they came to
a wooded vale head to many tetchy
wolves & Membyr was killed

Brutus went to france with a navy with him
& seeing a lot of fighting & killin of
people
came home & after that built a city over the
humber – called it york
jerussalem & silius latinus in italy
the prophets of israel & york went &
built
a fort & a castle with maids & twenty
years was he there these were the
names
of his sons: Brutus, Marerdud, Sisyll, Rys

Merud, Bleiddut, Iago, Bodlan, Kyngar
Gwawl, Dardan, Ior, Hector, Geraint
Runasser, Hywel & these were the names
the girls: Gloew, Geing, Ignonen, Eudaws
Gwenllian, Gwarrdyd, Angharad, Gwendoleu
Tagwystyl, Gorgon, Medlan, Methael
Eurar, Maelure, Camedra, Ragaw, Ecuba
Nestkein, Stadud, Ebren Blangan
Afallach, Angaes, Galaes the most
beautiful Gwerfil Pedwer, Eurdrych
Edrannor, Staydalt, Egron & york sent
them to Silius in italy & the sons
went to Germany & time told on them
& Silius had a port & they lived on this island
then came back brutus & his son Lleon after 10 years
peace was there & then a city was built in the north
& below a city called Caer lleon & in the
end of the age Selyf ap Dafydd built a temple
in Kaeryssalem & came queen Saba in her wisdom
& camc Silius & became king

5

page 3r (part of the Iliad)

nine when discovered troy
& he saw these princes there
the men of troy & the men of greece
& they fought first beat the men of greece
castor & pollux & everyone that was
similar & a joyful head of yellow hair
& big eyes & a pretty face
good was the form, body straight, long
Elen & her sistar similar, pretty was she
& obedient for that called was she
"Elen fanawg"
Menalaus the brother of the queen of Greece
& he was the genial, of a red
wonderful body
kymeredic, hegar was son of beleus king of
thetis
goddess of the seas wide deeps, cruel members
big suppery & pengrych yellow
& bravest nice arms & lovely face
& long browed ajax oileus of pedrogyl
was he
& the body of an eagle & funny was
he
Talamon said he & cruel against his enemies
& birthed a mule did he, black
Vlixes gwr llawen llawn brother
& a happy face & a resonable body
Diomedes, a strong man & pedrawgyl body
had he
& a saintly cruel face – the most
brilliant in battle
& a loud cry & a bad temper

Nestor a big, long, wise man, a white flesh to
him
Proteselaus a white, mellow, fast dedicated
man
Neocolonus a big inarticulate & a good face
& black eyes & skin
Palmedes was a long man, thin, gentle
Pilodarius was a fat man, tidy, sad
Machan was a big man, strong conspicuous,
sensible, mercyful
Meirion was a red man with a round body
moderate, insulting, cruel

Brisidia the wife of Agamemenon
short with white skin & blonde hair with dark brows
son of Priaf was gwyn pengrych & Members face
kind & suitable to love
Dephebus a stong man was he elenus a wise
kind man & fat he was & resembled a
dad in form & bearing
& different in temprament troilus a
large beautiful man
Alexander: long, white, pretty eyes, yellow hair
fine, a noble jaw, a genial voice
Aeneas a red, square proper stong of advice
big black eyes Antenor furr eyebrows
& sensible he was ecuba the wife of
briaf
the wife Fawrder & the eagle body & Andromalta
the wife of Hirwen with clear eyes
lovely & gentle was she: Casandra
moderate was she with small jaws
a prophetess Polixena wife of hirwen
ffurvid fynwfulhir & gentle eyes &
long
yellow hair fine brows & long fingers
& round legs & well formed feet were
to her
the she of her beauty that were excelled with
everyone

a generous mule was born to her
& then came a man, greek with a navy
with him

the country called athens first came Agamemnon
the city called mecene with a hundred ships
& memelus from the island called sporta with sixty ships with him
Athelas, Aphelas from phoecia they came

& ten ships & forty with them epitropus
from the country named polides
with forty ships with him
& limerus from the land called orchromeus
& thirty ships with them talamon o salmenia his
brother & princes with ten ships & twenty with them
Polunesmestor with twenty ships with them
Toas with forty ships with him
Ajax olieus from Lucris with eighteen ships on twenty
Venenas with thirty three ships
Antipus with eighteen on twenty ships
Jomenus with ninety ships
Vlixes with ten ships
Proteseaus with forty
Emelius with ten Potanius with forty four
Achil with thirty ships
Telebeleus with nine euriphilus with ten
Antipus with eleven ships
Pulibeces from larisa with forty ships
Diomedes of agripis with eighty ships
Pilotenus of meliboea with four
Genus of cipro with forty ships
Petroclus of venesia with forty ships
& Apenor with forty jnestius with thirty ships

page 12 line18 (again?)

a great snow was made under them

(user error)

g

hergest ward, ysbyty gwynedd, google translate, word 'spelling'

long	**53**	**12**	**25 44 12**
lat	**-4**	**9**	**39 08**

"≠"

column 53 12 col 25 line 44

vee deill anuon kenadeu
& did he herchi in wreak idaw
dywedut in the hat & the
gnawer & or dynast the rodeo
the verch idaw him without
argyfreu rents kan daroed idaw
the gyfoeth & non gold & he arrant the two girls others
& when gigleu aganipus tecket
the forwyn kyflawn vu of ei charyat
& dyedut & bot idaw
did he digawn of euro & aryant nat old & quite idaw him as nothing

but gwreic delediw dylyedawc
the caffeine children ohanei in etudes
ary kyfoeth & diannot
the kadarnhawyt the wedding
ac impend yspeit yg yrygtunt
kylch updated members of
the leicester there been exceeded the terms of the dofyon
kyuoeth
ahalassei by him drawls
through long time & the renascent
yrygtunt a did half & gymodloned

the kymerth maglawn
tywyssawc scotland leicester attaw
& segueing the bar mewl!
tag & him gewilid rack
bot by bot without varchogyon
vat in the osgord
& and then bot llyr in wed
that the tag & Maglawn
blyghau & oruc Cordeilla
rack hintage of varchogyon
teg & ex that & rack their servers
wynteu in teruysgu court
& dywedut & when the husband did bot
divan fair archaic on hugging teg
& ex that
& socio gulag
the rei others & and then
dywedut
"those in Leicester llidiaw &
oruc
& away, & Maglawn
& minuet hit earl kernyw

it comes to the other "
& derbyny didst of that
anrydedusny & benn has
the vlwydyn up darvu teruysc
that! rug their w/ asanaethwyr
& by that the sores guara
the verch vrthaw
& bade the varchogyon
the idea elegy wrath
eithyr five bar mwl & he
gwasanaethei & thristaw
aeth Llyr does then vawr
hyt & start ordinal elchwyl
to verch the oldest ides
of dybygu mercy ohonaei
wrthaw of ei maintain
& his varchogyon ygyt
& him being a leete did hitheu

by suffocating them heaven & the gyfoethnayar
                    than maffei of! long is the ony pear
                     all varchogyon the wrthaw
eithyr an that! teg & he gwasanaethei & dut nat dye
quite the old man keynote & bellow un

viii

column 12 **(part of the Iliad)**

minuet is right & the wind ymhoelut
rayed & vrenhin elite awlidemac there deuthant them & Agamemnon
& fu voodoo the fading as the
Diana fairness & arches
the gedymdeithon he ellwg
their llynges & cherdet zone
Troy & archers of philoten
in dywyssawc udunt & the hwnn
cathode the troy that!
teg & redynt husbands & in patho
interest elite argo odyno
the deuth him the land e lynges
the castle elite libels
& the hewn aged under amherodraeth
Priaf vrenhin & and then have the space
& their hanreith credit
pound rack they done

& the dyfot the isle
& profit it tandem
& the deuthant them ygyt

where the statistical headlines
Agamemnon the anreith
& call the tywyssogyon
in the gygor & did it
& odium kneaded to briaf
the wybot & vynnei he decrypt leech
& are anreith & degaussed alexander
& are kneaded & etiolate nyt alternative
diomedes & jluxes the vying to briaf
& when ytoed the kneaded

in ufydhau the orthygarch agamemnon
anfon & wnaethpwyt
&! celery the wlat
& the anreithaw elwit poesia

& to tevffras vrenhin the deuthant
& anreith
& gymerassant egg
& thevffras & depth
against them with a great power
bypath & achelarwy & dyrrawd
off the host hwnw
& his brathawd or
& then telepus and then hit him to the floor
he hamdiffynnwys rack the lad
achelarwy the commemoration
of the drwydet & gawssei him
& that he son! teg & erkwlff
the dat in court deuffras
coffee hefyt did rye lad of erkwlf
Diomedes vrenhin creulawn
the hwnn & old yfelu at that time on! nine him
& identifying all vrenhinyaeth the defrays
& by that bot telepus his son erkwlff
raises kanhorthwy idea
& then the tevffras knew dual than allied there
rack death of the sting of a rodassei
achelarwy ides & he vyw he
& rhodes vrenhinyaeth & wlat & elite bonsai the Telepus
the dead & and then king Telepus
& beris the buried in anrydedus & achelarwy when i got it
& Annor maintain the Telepus vrenhinyaeth new good arnaw
& dyfot in hidey that! teg
& wynteu the ymlad & husbands
lands Troy

Rachel & Thelephus
& dywawt when the bot nerthach

rodi bwyllyrneu of the masses
wheat from his kingdom he
hyt blwynyded minuet the fought of! honaw was the troy that!
teg & wind & felly
the presswylwys Telophus
&! celery or Odeon & ymhoelace
the island denedun to the masses
& anreith vawr ganja
& datkanawd the Agamemnon
& ego dymdeithon what fu
their kyfranc Agamemnon
& eye gedymdeithon & fu favorite
gamut this nay & emolassant
& those deuth the keen

ix

column 25 line 44

the teg & the ymladassant them wychyr lladassant he

column 4

in robust & it safe & arhoes time
welas fot when he will revenge
the very idaw dat he erchis dem
& attaw Antenor & dywawt
when the awmynnei elegy kannat
the oak ask the gun ias Greece
for the kammeu are insolence
a thoydynt idaw he does
nyt alternative noc ageu the dat
& dygedigaeth the sister
& area of Briaf and then order from the Anterior
minuet & he did & he & the log
deuth the place elwit Magnesia
att balldeus & he ex haruolles
Pelleus him & egad three
diwarnawt accommodation
& struction he pedwryd asked
sponsorship idaw what vynassei & Antenor & vene gave
& the hynn orchymynassei Briaf idaw
called up the Greeks edryt Esonia
& and then clybot of Belleus in the wrthrwm
kymerth he belonged on arnaw
of achaws of those arnaw him
& he erchis idaw adaw the land
& theruyneu on passage
& Antenor & went without ohir log
& odyna that duc him the progress

are wlat & elite Boccia & Salamania
& the deuth him to Alamo

beginning bade idaw & did send
esonja the & it's sister the briafedyt nat
very old maid of kynnal vrenhinawl
genedyl yg keithywet & Thalamon attethumb
& the Antenor & dywawt
than wnaethpwyt of ei bleit him
rwc in the butt of Briaf
but rodi Esonia idaw him
from the achaws dewret
& that's rodeo him anyone
& by that he & erchis the Antenor
& becomes the island
& Antenor or gyrchawd the log
& euth the land & elite Poesia
& odyno to Castor
& Colux diohir him
& making them very erchus

X

column 9

nine in the wheels hyt when rahat troy
a gwelet of honaw him tywyssogyon hynn here
when thei dagneued & chygreir that!
rwg men of troy & wax greek
& ryfot of! honaw he weitheu in
the hym tadeu them & Groec glybot ohonaw him
& what some bryt what
wren banyan agerydunt them
first Groec men speak of us Castor
Polux & all of a clyb the old fyffe
ilid molyannus bryt of hair peng
yellow groove & eyes great
& face-nice the good old ffuruf
a long bodies unyawn
Elen old sister Luana we
similar udunt them the old
hi beauty & ufyd the medwl
& Eskeirwreic good old
the age & place of rwg the dwyael
& therefore gelwit she "Elen fanawc"
thin & small idi age
Emnon tec body & big old idaw
& aelodeu stud duawl
& smart bonhedic old man kymen kyuo ethawc
Menelaus the vrawt vrenhined Groec
oethem exempt ell di

& his old man kymedrawl
of red arderchawc body
kymeredic hegar achil age
of the son of Beleus vrenhin of Metis
dwywes the moroed idaw corn

somewhat meaningful overlap with column 9

nine when discovered troy
& he saw these princes there
the men of troy & the men of greece
& they fought first beat the
men of Greece castor & Collux
& everyone that was
similar & a joyful head
of yellow hair
& big eyes & a pretty face
good was the form,
body straight, long
elen & her sistar similar,
pretty was she
& obedient for that
called was she "Elen fanawg"
Menalaus the brother
of the queen of greece
& he was the genial, of a
red wonderful body
kymeredic, hegar was
son of beleus king of thetis
goddess of the seas
wide deeps, cruel members
big suppery & pengrych yellow
& bravest nice arms & lovely face
& long browed Ejax oileus of pedrogyl
was he & the body
of an eagle & funny was he
Talamon said he & cruel against
his enemies & birthed a mule did he, black
Vlixes gŵr llawen llawn brother
& a happy face & a resonable body
Diomedes, a strong man
& pedrawgyl body had he
& a saintly cruel face
the most brilliant in battle
& a loud cry & a bad temper
nestor a big, long, wise man, a white flesh to him Proteselaus a white,
mellow, fast dedicated man
Neocolonus a big inarticulate
& a good face
& black eyes & skin
Palmedes was a long man, thin, gentle
Pilodarius was a fat man, tidy, sad
machan was a big man, strong conspicuous sensible, mercyful
Meirion was a red man with a round body
moderate, insulting, cruel
Brisidia the wife of agamemenon
short with white skin & blonde hair with dark brows son of Priaf
was gwyn pengrych & Members face
kind & suitable to love
dephebus a stong man was he elenus a wisekind man & fat he
was & resembled a dad in form & bearing
& different in temprament troilus a large beautiful man
Alexander: long, white, pretty eyes, yellow hair
fine, a noble jaw, a genial voice
eneas a red, square proper stong of advice
big black eyes Antenor furr eyebrows

old dwyuron wide & aduwyndrych
& are aelodeu creulawn greduawl;
great llathredic & hair pengrych
yellow gwaredawc as weak
& the bravest mywn arueu
& surface hyfryt & long ages
& generous Eiax of Lileus aged man pedrogyl
eagle idaw body
& aelodeu greduawl kadarn
a funny old man Talamon clear voice
years to come
& husband greduawl
creulawn against elynyon
& annwyt mul gantaw
brigeir top black & curled
Vlixes full of joyful husband
& kadarn vrat surface & joyful
& body kymedrawl kymen
& ygnat old diomedes husb
& kadarn & body pedrawgyl idaw
& surface adfwyn create full
& finest in ymlad loud voice
hennyd & in hot rwc & valiant old
nestor great man long width wise
& chnawt white idaw proteselaus husb
& mirror speedy white adfwyn good ymdiret grit
neocolonus great man pryerus
llidiawc bloesc & surfaced round
llygeit black & aelodeu great
palamedes old man long mein
clare & ygnat great! vrydus
milodarius old man print greduawl
syberw sad machan old big man
kadarn hyspys smart ofnawc
truga mwl meiryon old man red
& brawl rounded body kyme age
idaw sarhaedus worm creulawn
nyt old amynedus Brisidia:
gwreic agamemnon old ffurtheyd
nyt years long & chnawt white
& me hair lake & aeleu black

& llygeit llathreit advwyn
& body kyfyawn & dywedwydat clare kwyilydy
chaff & anwyt mule neck pryt men of troy
& iaf vren dam plywychwn rack
hin troy great man ages & face-tec idaw
voice & genial & the body of an eagle hector

39 line 08 is land yummy, do cravings kid

k

bod leian library
(place [of the] nun)

longditude	**51**	**45**	**15 5226**
latitude -1	**15**	**15 141**	

"≠"

pages	**51r**	**45**	**15 line 52**
	1	**15**	**15 line 14**

jesus 111 (red book of hergest) page 51r (column 202)

byr is the elynyon & kylchynu the vye
dinoed own & phy enemy bynac
fi & a separate meet him
& gay for chledyf the building
& so of pop zone in the bydei arthur
ag neuthur aerua kanys geitheu
not the dominant brytan geitheu
others that they prevail against the romans

& that is when yttoedynt the bragart
without wybot py! not the dam einei the vudu
golyaeth nachaf morud earl fort loy
in dyuot & r leg & your edassam us
the seed uchot yg g ersyll & deissy
fyt in kyrchu their gelynyon is not!
been run warning of r lies behind them
& mynet drostunt by their g asgaru
& gwneuthur air ua ry meint dirfa

& then the syrthas saint lla order

203

by land! fa rag ynuan the formany
by the then didst where the n m ent kid on the non
deheu not the house clad in enrydedus
wrought!
lla the wall kei & psu house in urathedic
hyt kam complaint & the kastell nathoed he itself
ny where he forsaketh so far yny vu uar of kei
the sting of he & the forest old & there goes the man
Manachla ac ermitwyr of Enryded

& the earl changi dylyei the claddyt
hodlyn house nyssa capsu yt hyt city he
own the older elir the tyruan
where the clad house others & the gyrda
erchis arthur in their manachlogoed until
saf udunt on hyt complaint latoed
& then the corn erchis him that the wlat cladu the enemies
& anuon wellness amhera break hyt sened Rome
& bade mene dog udunt than dylyynt ie teyrnget
oh nys prydein no alternative where he arthur
overcome the mcas in regain the dinassoed

& when yttoed summer beginning dyuot
& arthur will stick /w mountain mynheeurth vynet zone
Rufein nachaf genadeu pry isl& of the Arthur
Lundein in menegi ry daruot the vedra house
nei fab overcome the airdnys risca
crown of britain to the kingdom for the long-e
own wickedness & the dr brat a would draw
genh direc vrenhines of e riein cadeir thery sleep
rent polluting kyf reith d mod ly neithoryeu
a forsaketh menegi that g is the arthur the place peidya

& oruc & evnet potential for the rufein
& ymchoelut zone & the island of britain
& brenhined the ynyssed that! teg & him
& Howel son of Emyr with cell
& manta host the tangnefedu & hedychu
& complaint ladoed kanys the yscymunedickaf vrad tar by vedra

& anuonassei cheldric house nyssa cy, england
& hyt germania the gynulla the masses & most
& gallei gateway ida & identify & udunt
& oruc of humyr hyt y Scotlont & you are anec kymeint
& fuassei & the hors heingyst kynno those yg kent
& that rith & yth cent deuth cheldric no interest in llas

1

page 45r column 178

a forsaketh datkanu the letter rack almost arthur
& are brenhined & tywyssogyon & oedynt that!
nice & him he & their nets & went the!
teg hyt try the gymryt kyghor py ri ke what
nelhynt against kymyne not be so ual
& the corn oedynt in esgynnu gradeu tar
kad the earl kerny even as the group ila ued
en la the ymadra d honey are number one
kynm hynn ask are! that has been to me
rack goruot of lesged the brytanyeit long crowd

& losing their clot thousand rye went
of honn they dealt hye! glurach's butt is one
of the genedloed holla I being on the sly
in the place peitter & Arueru of Arueu
& aruer of rhdbyll & taplas
& love graged nyt tentative
there is no contamination of lace
ged pwy what bynhac arz ner emerged
from there & chedernit & enryded & lot
kanys five mlyned hayach & r ethynt
when yttym us in the larueru rand seguryt
funny & without arueru of non yll in
lad & hen that the black stick an rydhau us
llesged & that is an exciting against the Rufein
hyt when we would describe an clot & non
thousand ryaeth the old gynefa
forsaketh with your edut the battlefield of the ymadro
lyon those lla order from rei others
of their nets & updated members
deuthant there eistedfa are
& forsaketh seating from which of the place

Arthur & fal hynn rthunt a house
vyg kedymdeithon on the corn
& the complex molyant rei hyt
that & raise their kyghoreu & their thousand
ryaeth & arr! honn of un vryt roddant kyghor
& wise rack! vedyly what fo ia ny atteb
against the attebyon hynn kanys py what bynhac a rack!
ve dylyer is good so that by yesterday
thon when del on the eithret has vyd
diodef & hen that has

179

that the gun ninheu diodef war ru line
if a common denomination wise & putted
gyghor in the racuedyly pywed gahanu
& that we may be battle their nets &
challenge the war most closely resembles the corn
nyt ma r quite in the ofynhau kanys an!
dylyedus they ie commanding tea
yrnget of the island of britain
kanys didst dylyu the house he & ida pay him
hen the host of ulkassar tag & the others
forsaketh him & so on & anuuns
teruysc the deb! rag an old!
ateu ninheu & the black passant s rufein
honn & the island of preis
complaint they became tretha

& hen that py what bynhac i get short or zyll than
chedernit nyt of dylyet the kynhellir hunn
the bynhac pcl & pek preis an thing!
dylyedus & the eis education maintenance
for a non! dylyedus ent of the ma keissa teyrnget
the i hym not in gynhebic & the so ninheu
deissyf n teyrnget the gantunt hyo ru line
& rkadarnaf of! honom us kymeret of the other
kanys of r overcome ys ulkassar
& others amherodron gave his house island of britain
& of those on the son! honn question teyrnget of!

hanei in gynhebic the so minheu & varnst dylyu of Rufein
pay the min teyrnget sowing
kanys vy parents ynheu faster
& oresgynnassant Rufein
& kynhal passant nyt alternative fab
comprehensive
wall balls ganhorth the bran by the vrat duke
borg is forsaketh gog hung petwar
ystyl on hugeint of dylyedogyon

Rufein rack near the fort & he dalyassant
dorla the order of amseroed
& forsaketh those custenin son leech
& Maxen son Llywelyn of all vn rei in
car near the mine from gerenhyd
& vrenhined arderchanys co the crown of
britain
the forsaketh the vnag ilyd & gassant amherodraeth Rufein
that pony bern & rth ch ch to bot ia nyminheu
deissyfeit tyrant get a rufein from ffreinc
& are ynyssed others ny rutheb us udunt the king

page15 line 52

gelynyon & then ymchoelut their ely

13

jesus 111 (red book of hergest) page 1 verso

Also Iliad

& troy hyt night & the deuthant hithe
the are land & then the odd
dugassant erk if & thelaon
& Pheleus their forces out of ex llogeu
& ada ssant pastor & pholux
& the nestor of myn llogeu
& so ystryac odyna the datkan this house
& blight the ny laomedon vrenhin Troy
rydyuot llyges of the uor segun
the oec drlat him being a stolen from him

& amylder of varchogyon the!
teg & he dyuot the are where corn oedynt hya
beginning ymlad & the erk lf or athoed
the castle elit to lium
& rei ynuydyon aue melas him
there without dru ymoglut
& the beginning of the slaughter
& then all of the interior
datkan the house loamdown ryost gelyny
a rainbow on him the castle Ilium
gwedhy & while he corne shackle
ymhoeles or interior & there
& di the Groec in the the against
& derk ada lf him Talamon or in the first went
arkas hunn the men tell the hno achaos the dered him
Rhodes esoniam girl laomedon vre ass
the rei others all or odynt veibyon the laomedon

& blue nyt & alternative neophilus

clius & ampiter Priaf vab laomedon
& yttoed in time ea
where else in the gossodyssei?
it for me erk or lf dathoedynt that!
teg & he gymerassant anreith va are
& ex dugant of their llogeu home & ody
than the corn ymchoelassant huh
& Thalamon or duke esoniam ygyt & him

& then when the house datkan Briaf wry the lad tattoo
ex fort & the in the anreith fadra desoniam
thed air roessei erk lf & the dalamon
garos gut Troy in marat ydus
& those of the Groec trwm the kymerth it on me
& tell Ilium & sourcing nasty in respect of service
& the ecuba reic ygyt & he ei feibon nyt alternative

Hector & Alexander & Deiphebus & Elenus & Troilus

& Androsac & Cassandra & Pholixena the verch
& meibon of orderchadeu hefyt the others!
teg & him buyssynt uar meibon others to!
good of him over the derchadeu

didst shall be thy ny hanuot of genedyl vrenhina lo!

& gisa Briaf forsaketh order from the Antenor
mynet & stolen from him & he
& the log deuth the the place el magnesia
Attitbel deus & he haruolles
Pelleus him handed & three free accommodation
it & raped ford struction him ovyn than dida
what vynassei & Antenor & venegis & the hynn
orchymynassei briaf ida called up
the groec edryt esonia & and then clybot
of belleus in thrum kymerth he belonged
at me from on of so me him

& he erchis the ida ada lat
& he theruyneu on passage
& antenor & went without ohir log

& odyna that duc him the progress
are wlat & el it boccia & salamania
& the deuth him to talamon ida began to call up
& anuon stolen from the esonja chair briaf
& thy edyt nat age of sea ice n kynnal vrenhin

        al genedyl yg keithy et a thalamon

& atted what the Antenor
& athy to not naethpwyt of
dr bleit him in the butt of briaf
        but rodi esonia ida him on that
        de ret & that rodei him anyone
& that he & hen erchis the antenor
& good of the isl& & antenor
                or lift up your log & deuth the rwlat
& el it poenia & odyno to castor &
& colux diohir he erchus uenit rye neuthur ia ny Briaf
& edryt esonia that dida air it & castor & colux
        or saint than your edas naethoydynt vn step

page 15v

(deleted through mercy to the reader)

page 15 line14

kestyll & dinassoed of ease itself

www.ingramcontent.com/pod-product-compliance
Lightning Source LLC
Chambersburg PA
CBHW060928170426
43193CB00023B/2986
* 9 7 8 1 9 1 2 2 1 1 1 7 3 *